CORPORATE CHRISTIAN *101*

A BELIEVER'S GUIDE TO **SURVIVING** *CORPORATE AMERICA*

VALERIE LYNN RUSSELL

Corporate Christian 101

Copyright © 2022 by Valerie Lynn Russell

Published by Arcane Publishing, LLC
First printing, October, 2022

ISBN: 978-1-7348638-5-7 (Paperback)
ISBN: 978-1-7348638-6-4 (Ebook)

Valerie Lynn Russell, Author
Jennifer Calhoun, Editor
LaToya K. Bilbo, Writer of Foreword

Book design by Chris Drabenstott, Arcane Publishing, LLC
Cover design by Goldin Productions

All rights reserved. This book may not be reproduced in whole or in part, stored in a retrieval system, or transmitted in any form or by any means—electronic, mechanical, digital, photocopy, recording, or any other—without written permission from the publisher, except by a reviewer, who may quote brief passages in a review.

DEDICATION

I dedicate this book to my parents, Annie-Jean Elliott and Wayne Russell.

My father started working when he was only seven years old. He was no stranger to hard work and the benefits it could bring. With a limited education, he started his own funeral business and grew it into a thriving operation. He taught me you should never sit back and wait for someone to hand you something. I learned to never make excuses and that, no matter how hard the challenge is, you need to get the job done. Dad instilled in me the values and principles of having a strong work ethic and taught me how to be self-sufficient. These values can seem hard to come by today.

My mother, Annie-Jean Elliot, was a hard worker, too. She was also a great homemaker and a fantastic cook. After my parents divorced, she worked at a factory to help raise my brother and me. She was committed and dedicated to her craft, her work, and her children.

Raised in the Baptist church, both my parents provided me with a strong foundation and the Christian principles that helped me believe in myself, overcome life's challenges, and become the best person I could be at home and in the workplace.

So, I dedicate this book to you, Mom and Dad. I will always love you. Rest in peace.

TABLE OF CONTENTS

Foreword	ix
Preface	xi
Acknowledgments	xiii
Introduction	xv

PRINCIPLE 1
Prepare for Your Day with God's Armor — 1

PRINCIPLE 2
Set the Atmosphere for Work — 13

PRINCIPLE 3
Redirect Office Gossip — 25

PRINCIPLE 4
Maintain Your Integrity and Keep the Faith — 35

PRINCIPLE 5
Live at Peace with Everyone — 55

PRINCIPLE 6
Let God Handle Your Seasons and Setbacks — 65

PRINCIPLE 7
　Overcome Fear with Faith　　　　　　　75

PRINCIPLE 8
　Be Free of Unhealthy Competition　　　87

PRINCIPLE 9
　Prepare for Your Promotion　　　　　　99

PRINCIPLE 10
　Rest in God　　　　　　　　　　　　　111

Conclusion　　　　　　　　　　　　　　　121
About Valerie Lynn Russell　　　　　　　　125

FOREWORD

As a spiritual sister of Valerie Russell, I am ecstatic, humbled, and honored about presenting her work to you. I met Valerie through the In Pursuit of Me (IPOM) community. Our first close encounter was being roomies at an IPOM weekend women's retreat. Not only were we roomies, but we were also both born in sweet home Alabama.

In *Corporate Christian 101*, Valerie has done an exceptional job capturing foundational principles to help Christian believers thrive in the corporate workplace. Her book has truly blessed me as a civilian working for the government and in ministry. Valerie has developed tenets that are not only relevant to Corporate America but to other work environments as well.

The relatable short stories in this book will captivate you and cause you to step back and consider your own experiences. They will grab your attention and curiosity, giving you a springboard to overcome the hurdles and obstacles in the work environment. The contemplation questions are thought-provoking, providing space for you to reflect on your own actions, reactions, and behaviors.

In this book, Valerie vulnerably allows you to see corporate America through her own personal experiences, the experiences of the characters in her stories, then explores what God has to say about it using biblical scriptures. *Corporate Christian 101* will help you effectively integrate her valuable principles in any work environment.

Through her writing, experience, wisdom, and knowledge, Valerie helps you prepare for your day, feeling empowered to conquer any problem that comes your way. If you've struggled with toxic work environments, office gossip, maintaining your integrity, handling setbacks, unhealthy competition, restlessness, and more, this book is for you!

LaToya K. Bilbo, Inspirational Life Speaker
Created by Words, LLC

PREFACE

Throughout my 20-plus years working in corporate America, I've met many people from different backgrounds. Many of these people were Christians. Oftentimes, they were drawn to me, seeking advice on how to overcome corporate politics while maintaining their Christian principles. There was one man, however, who was the main inspiration for me to write this book.

Everyone knew he was a Christian, but no one knew the magnitude of his internal struggles. We were working on a job together, and he quit suddenly and unexpectedly. *I never saw him again.* I later found out he took a gun and began shooting at random cars from a bridge before ending his own life.

After that tragic incident, some colleagues at work shared that he'd been struggling with depression. *I never knew.* All I knew was that we were both Christian believers and loved God. I couldn't help but wonder what might've happened if I had spent more time getting to know him. Maybe I could have shown him the only presence of Jesus he may have seen that day through a smile, hug, or an encouraging word. I asked God to never let me miss an opportunity to be a beacon of His love to someone in the workplace or anywhere.

I made the commitment to be a representative of Christ in the workplace from that moment forward. It's God's assignment for me to help anyone who's struggling to maintain their Christian principles in corporate America. God has made provisions for us exactly where we are, so there is no need to feel stressed or burdened.

My hope is that the principles in this book will serve as inspirational reminders that you have everything you need to overcome challenges in the workplace when you use God's Word as your weapon. I wrote this book for you, the woman or man of God who works in corporate America. God has already made provisions for you to achieve abundantly and successfully. May your journey lead you to thrive and live a life of prosperity and joy.

ACKNOWLEDGMENTS

I first want to thank my Lord and Savior Jesus Christ for choosing me and putting me on this assignment to bless other people through my testimonies and experiences.

To Stephanie Kirkland, my mentor—my sister in Christ, you've aided me on my journey by helping me pull up bad roots in my life, working with me to map out the blueprint of where I want to go, and helping me understand my "why."

To Barnell Lytton, thank you for teaching me how to love unconditionally and showing me how to love those who are oftentimes hard to love.

To Joyce Murphy and Lynda Young, thank you for being my angels in corporate America. You watched me cry, guided me, coached me, lifted me up, and prayed for me.

To Frank Lacomba, you are my brother. Throughout corporate America, you made me laugh, think, and helped me process things I didn't understand.

To Vicky Siragusa, you are my sister. Thank you so much for being that friend who taught me things I wouldn't have been exposed to in corporate America. Thank you for loving me and having patience with me along the way; I will be forever grateful.

To Nancy Johnson, you are my "shero." You inspire me in how you run and manage your businesses, as well as how you continue to educate and help others. I can only pray that God gives me just a morsel of your strength, beauty, and talent. As I continue to grow, I appreciate you more and more for loving me, for your patience and kindness, and for your generosity in helping me on my journey. Thank you.

INTRODUCTION

During my years as a working professional, I've watched believers literally lose their faith, their jobs, and even their lives because of the challenges of working in corporate America. We spend most of our time at work, so it's essential to put on the full armor of God to be able to stand against the wiles of the enemy. 1 Peter 5:8 tells us the enemy "prowls around like a roaring lion looking for someone to devour." We need to stay alert!

Our place of work is where we create the means to secure our livelihood. It affects where we live, eat, shop, and how we educate our families. Our jobs play an integral part in the quality of life we create for ourselves. Sure, we have family time and enjoy our weekends. On Sunday mornings, many enjoy corporate praise and worship with like-minded people. It's a beautiful feeling when you're free to worship and everything is in complete harmony. But what happens to that harmonious feeling when you go back to the grind? What happens to the "Great God" when your boss says something ugly or disrespectful to you? Is it not the same God who is in control of everything and who blessed you with this job?

As believers in Christ, it's important to know who we are in Him—to understand our position, our purpose, and our power. Sometimes we feel we are standing alone, left to endure situations that seem as though we're walking through the valley of the shadow of death. Fear not; God is walking with you. When we focus on the valley, we forget who's by our side. We react, get upset, and even lose control at times. I know, I've been there. There will always be challenges in the workplace and in life in general, yet some challenges can make you feel as though you are about to go underwater and surely drown. Remember, you are here on assignment by our almighty God. When you are tested, don't give up!

Satan is watching and listening to the words you say to others and to yourself. You can expect tests and distractions to challenge your faith. Satan's mission is to kill, steal, and destroy your joy, but God has placed you where you are for a reason, and He has a divine purpose for your job and your life. No matter what you do or where you work, you can be a blessing to everyone you interact with, giving them your best.

You are about to explore ten Christian-based principles that will help you survive and thrive in corporate America. Each principle includes personal stories, applicable scriptures, and an opportunity for you to journal about your own experiences in the workplace.

I've met and learned from many Christian believers with varied backgrounds and struggles whose stories lie in the pages ahead. Their names have been changed and their stories are told from my perspective. As you read the stories and study related scriptures, I pray they inspire you and assist you in creating a more peaceful, empowering, and productive work environment.

Are you ready? Let's get started.

PRINCIPLE 1

Prepare for Your Day with God's Armor

> *"Put on all of God's armor so that you will be able to stand firm against all strategies of the devil. For we are not fighting against flesh-and-blood enemies, but against evil rulers and authorities of the unseen world, against mighty powers in this dark world, and against evil spirits in the heavenly places."*
>
> *(Ephesians 6:11-12)*

What is the first thing you do when you wake up in the morning? Most people are quick to grab their phone to check missed calls or text messages and scroll through social media. Many people lie in bed thinking about their to-do list and what they didn't get accomplished the day before.

The first thing you do when you wake up sets the tone for the day. This means you must prepare yourself for spiritual warfare. Before you hop out of bed and begin your day, develop a routine of spending some time with God through prayer and reading His Word. If you don't currently read the

Bible, there are many versions to choose from; find a version that's engaging and easy for you to understand. Feed your spirit the Good News to empower yourself with positivity and confirmation. As you face challenges throughout the day, you can call upon the power of the Word you've placed in your spirit.

Landon

Landon worked in a high-paying and highly demanding sales position. He enjoyed benefiting from perks like free concert tickets and fancy suites at football games, but he struggled managing the pressure of his job. Emotionally, there were days he felt happy and fulfilled, but most of the time he felt stressed and agitated.

Landon was consistently late for work. His mornings often began with threatening text messages from his ex, calls from family members asking him for money, or calls from creditors. By the time Landon arrived at work, he was already mentally drained. His energy was typically low from dealing with outside influences which affected his ability to be productive. These negative influences not only affected Landon's productivity at work, but they also negatively impacted his peace, sleep, and overall health. Before the age of 50, he had already suffered two heart attacks. He'd recovered and eventually returned to work, but his old patterns continued. Landon spent a large part of his career feeling unhappy and ruled by his job.

PRINCIPLE 1 | Prepare for Your Day with God's Armor

Rather than living the abundant life God wanted for him, he was simply existing, trying to get by from one day to the next. Landon loved God. While he had prayed for the job he was hired for, he struggled to thrive because he continually allowed the stress in his life to steal his joy. When faced with challenges at work, he began to question if the job was really for him. Day in and day out, Landon carried his stress around like a backpack. It began to take its toll on his health, productivity, and relationships. What began as work-related stress and anxiety became a part of Landon's entire life, affecting his friends, family, and everyone he was close with. He started to hate his job, blaming it for his unhappiness and cursing God for his struggles.

What Landon failed to do was properly prepare for his day by putting on the armor of God and giving gratitude for his job and all the blessings in his life. By the end of each day, he was depleted with nothing left to give to the people he loved other than complaints. From the time he arrived home to the time he went to bed, his thoughts were consumed by everything that went wrong that day, causing him to feel restless, burned out, and exhausted. He was on a hamster wheel of negativity he couldn't get off, which was exactly what Satan wanted!

"Listen to my voice in the morning, Lord. Each morning I bring my requests to you and wait expectantly."
(Psalm 5:3)

Yesterday is the past, and today is a new day filled with God's endless grace and mercies. God promises that he will always be with us. Preparing for your day requires spending time reading the Bible, learning about His love for you, and claiming the power He has given you to overcome difficult circumstances. We all lead busy lives, but the more time you spend with God, the more equipped you will become to live in fulfillment and abundance. You will begin to notice changes in how you react to life's obstacles and challenges. Putting on the full armor of God requires you to develop a level of faith and knowing that every day is a good day. Why? Because you're alive!

Every unforeseen challenge will work for your highest good, but you must have faith. Hebrews 11:1 tells us "Faith shows the reality of what we hope for; it is the evidence of things we cannot see." If you are reading this book while sitting in a chair, you have faith that the chair will hold you. In fact, the support and stability of that chair probably never even crossed your mind. How would you feel having that much faith in God's ability to support you in overcoming any attack of the enemy? God did not give us the spirit of fear; rather, He gave us power, love, and a sound mind.

HOW TO PREPARE FOR YOUR DAY BY PUTTING ON GOD'S ARMOR

Pray and Meditate

Starting your day with prayer is the most powerful way to set the tone for each day. Committing to at least ten minutes per day can make a massive difference by reducing stress and bringing peace and relaxation to your body and mind. Physical ailments are often a symptom of mental distress, and prayer and meditation can help you foster more vibrant health. Through daily prayer and meditation, you can experience more happiness and peace of mind, improved concentration, and increased faith in God.

With these tools, you proactively offer God a "thank you" for His constant, eternal love, grace, and support. Before you roll out of bed, allow for some time to give God thanks for waking you up and providing you with another day to live. In Ephesians, we learn that God's desire is for us to pray on all occasions with all kinds of prayers and requests. If you're not sure what to pray for, start by giving thanks for what He has *already* done in your life, as well as what you believe and expect He can do for you today and in your future. Start a gratitude journal and write brief "thank you" notes to God. Christianity is about building an intimate relationship with God. There is no right or wrong way to pray and communicate with God; all that matters is that He is listening.

Sing

Sing a song to the Lord. Now, before you skip over this section, hear me out! Although some people find joy in humming a little tune in the shower or while making morning coffee, no one's expecting you to belt out a hymn as soon as you wake up. But for a moment, think about how it feels when you hear your favorite song. Singing can stir your soul, creating an opportunity to have an intimate moment with God. If you don't know what song to sing, think of some of the things you're grateful for and sing your gratitudes to God—that's right, just make it up as you go! You may discover you can carry more of a tune than you think.

Read the Bible

Read a scripture or two. You don't have to be a Bible scholar to hear a message through God's Word. You only need to have the desire to get closer to Him, and He will meet you where you are. You can start from the beginning or just open it up to any page and trust that the message you receive is exactly what you needed to hear. God's holy Word is alive, and it will speak to whatever is going on in your life. For example, if you're having trouble managing stress, your solution might be found in Philippians 4:6: "Don't worry about anything; instead, pray about everything. Tell God what you need and thank Him for all He has done." This scripture speaks simply and directly

PRINCIPLE 1 | Prepare for Your Day with God's Armor

to that feeling of anxiety. Your faith in the working power of God's Word will allow it to sink into your spirit and ease your stress. Reading scripture is the best way to prepare yourself for victory over any obstacle. God has already prepared new blessings and mercies that are waiting for you to receive.

Daily spiritual preparation is so important. The book of Ephesians reminds us to be strong in the Lord and in His mighty power. We must put on God's full armor so we can stand firm against all strategies of the devil. The spirit of the enemy is always among us, so we must be on guard. God expects us to show up and give it our all every day. He holds us accountable in our stewardship whether on the job or off. Inside or outside of the workplace, as a Christian steward, you can be prepared by taking your stewardship responsibilities seriously and preparing for them daily. God is the creator and owner of all good things. All that is possessed comes as a gift from His Holy hands, and those gifts are abundant if you're ready to accept them.

Now that you have been given some examples of how to spiritually prepare for the day, it's time for you to take charge! Don't wake up another day dreading your work or allowing outside forces to kill your spirit and your joy. The enemy does not want you to know that you have power over what may be a toxic environment, but as you will see throughout the pages ahead, you have God's full power to defeat any attempts of the enemy. In the same way you have faith the sun will rise and set every day; you must have that same faith in knowing that no

7

spiritual plan that is formed against you will prosper. Decide to command your morning to be peaceful and your day to be victorious. The power is in your hands to start each new day with a fresh anointing from God. It doesn't matter what happened the day before, and tomorrow will take care of itself. One day at a time, implementing these consistent practices will equip you to handle any situation with confidence and peace in corporate America and in life.

JOURNAL

Contemplations

- ✝ What are your current daily practices to communicate with God?
- ✝ What is your current morning routine to spiritually prepare for the day? What practices could you add to build a closer relationship with God?
- ✝ List five things you are looking forward to accomplishing today at work.
- ✝ Which scriptures resonate with you to help you overcome challenges in the workplace? (Following are some scriptures to choose from.)

Scriptures to Reference

Ephesians 6:10-18 — "A final word: Be strong in the Lord and in his mighty power. Put on all of God's armor so that you will be able to stand firm against all strategies of the devil.

Psalm 5:3 — "Listen to my voice in the morning, Lord. Each morning I bring my requests to you and wait expectantly."

Psalm 118:24 — "This is the day that the Lord has made. We will rejoice and be glad in it."

PRINCIPLE 2

Set the Atmosphere for Work

"The tongue can bring death or life; those who love to talk will reap the consequences."

(Proverbs 18:21)

Now that you've prepared for your day with the help of God's armor, you will want to set a positive atmosphere for your workday. The spirit can change quickly with unplanned distractions like busy traffic, an angry text message, or unconscious stress you may be conjuring in your mind about the day that lies ahead. The truth is, your workplace culture has a major impact on your productivity and mental health both at work as well as at home, so it's imperative to be proactive in setting the atmosphere with an intentional attitude of love and positivity.

In the book of Genesis, God created the elements of the world by breathing life into them. You too have the power to bring good things into your work setting. For example, if you want to experience more joy, try posting positive affirmations in your workspace and speak them silently or out loud. You can bring peace, victory, and love into your atmosphere just by believing your desires will appear.

Before diving into work, ask God for the wisdom to help you solve any problems or issues that come your way. He is always with you, so don't hesitate to have a little talk with Him throughout the workday as if He was sitting right there in front of you. The tone you set at work—how you want to feel and contribute—begins and ends with you; it's your responsibility to create the kind of environment you most want to experience.

Michelle and Angie

Michelle worked as senior cashier at a major grocery store chain. In the beginning, she loved her job, but as time passed, she began to witness many of the other employees engaging in constant judgment and gossip about each other, their customers, and new corporate policies.

The staff expressed their lack of support for the new corporate initiatives through bickering amongst each other and being disrespectful toward management. As the environment became increasingly more toxic, turnover increased, and Michelle was quickly losing her desire to come to work. The joy she once felt for her job turned into stress and eventually depression, although she continued to work there for several more years. The weariness Michelle carried about her job

PRINCIPLE 2 | Set the Atmosphere for Work

affected her health and happiness in a way she didn't even fully realize.

One day, Michelle met Angie, who was recently hired at the store. Angie was a vibrant older woman with a unique presence. There was something about Angie's positive energy and warm countenance that made others want to be around her. For years, Michelle and Angie worked together despite the continued bickering and unrest of the other employees. It was refreshing for Michelle to be around such a sincere, loving woman who appeared to carry her happiness on the inside, unaffected by external situations. As the two were talking one day, Michelle confronted Angie about how she always seemed to remain so positive in such a toxic environment. She asked, "How do you manage to not get sucked into the complaining, gossip, and bickering and maintain such a pleasant disposition every day?"

Angie grinned and said, "I can't control the attitudes and actions of others, but with God's help I always have control over how I respond, both internally and externally." She added that God was her refuge in times of need, so when she witnessed other employees engaging in negative behaviors, she found her peace by speaking and affirming the powerful and uplifting Word of God. When she saw others huddled together gossiping, she just avoided them and silently spoke a positive affirmation or two to calm herself and the atmosphere.

This changed Michelle's entire perspective about her job. She decided to adopt some of Angie's affirmations and modeled the way she carried herself. Taking back control of her attitude and the way she responded to the negative situations going on around her immediately changed how she felt inside. In creating a more positive atmosphere for herself, Michelle noticed the same change happening throughout the company.

"This is the day the Lord has made. We will rejoice and be glad in it."

(Psalm 118:24)

I know a lot of people who say they aren't morning people. "Don't talk to me until I've had at least two cups of coffee." They shuffle into work slowly with their head hanging, slugging their briefcase along, and closing the door behind them as soon as they hit their office.

Whether working in an office or online, you don't have to be a morning person to create a positive atmosphere. Choosing your attitude and speaking uplifting words to yourself may require some sincere, consistent effort to create a morning routine around your emotional state. One of the hardest things to change is your routine because you've unconsciously been doing the same things over and over throughout your life, and likely getting the same results. If you're not a morning person, consider creating a new routine that happens before you dive into work. It may not feel natural at first, and change doesn't happen overnight, but in time you'll find it can gradually improve your life.

PRINCIPLE 2 | Set the Atmosphere for Work

Although the story of Michelle and Angie happened at a physical workplace, many people still have trouble managing a peaceful work environment while working from home. The increased number of people working virtually has created a whole new set of workplace issues. Working remotely can cause employees to feel isolated from one another and separated from their managers. It has become more difficult and less personal to communicate directly and working virtually can create hidden or unseen "office drama." Working remotely makes it easier for people to shut down, burn out, or ignore stressful situations, but you can still be a catalyst to improve the atmosphere by expressing your leadership and positivity through uplifting and empowering words.

You may not have the ability to close the door behind you once you get to work. If your workspace is next to or near someone who hates their job, you need to be even more intentional to protect and maintain your atmosphere. Just like Michelle and Angie, you have a choice as to which energy you are affected by—yours or someone else's. Creating that morning routine to get yourself into the proper state of mind is even more important when your job requires you to share close proximity with another for long periods of time. You may choose to limit the amount of conversation you have with them or, if they're open to it, share some helpful tips on how you choose to set the atmosphere for your day through positivity, power, and peace.

> *"Don't copy the behavior and customs of this world, but let God transform you into a new person by changing the way you think. Then you will learn to know God's will for you, which is good and pleasing and perfect."*
>
> *(Romans 12:2)*

Have you ever worked for a manager who was like Dr. Jekyll and Mr. Hyde? Sometimes, you just don't know who you're going to be dealing with. If this is the case, remember who you are as a sovereign child of God and hold your ground. Like Angie learned, you can't control other people or the situations that occur around you, but you can remain in your peace. If you've properly prepared yourself for the day and set your own atmosphere, you can shift your focus from the unpredictable behaviors of others and, instead, zero in on what God has equipped you to do. God has given you endurance and peace of mind to handle any situation, and you were blessed with where you are right now in your career. It may be hard to see at the moment, but the way you continue to walk in love and peace serves as a living example to others.

There are many examples cited in the Bible showing how speaking affirmative words changes the entire outcome of a difficult situation. Whether working somewhere onsite or remotely, it's very easy to succumb to an unhealthy work environment; just remember you have the power inside of you to change it!

HOW TO SET THE ATMOSPHERE AT WORK

Pray for Productivity Over Your Day

Before launching yourself into the workday, take a minute to relax yourself and pray. After taking a deep breath, remind yourself of your goals and what you hope to achieve for the day. This will make it mentally easier to get through even the roughest of mornings. Talk to God about how you want your day to go and keep it positive. Don't focus on problems that happened yesterday or ones that could happen tomorrow. Instead, adopt the attitude that today is a new day and God is with you. If you feel strong in His love, you will be strong. That will make it easier to solve problems and walk away from petty drama. Remember what I said about sitting down in a chair and trusting it to hold you? Well, imagine the sturdiest, most well-made chair in the universe and plopping right down in it—God's got you like that, so trust in Him!

Create a Morning Routine

Write out how you want your day to look, whether it's a journal entry or a simple list. Writing things down helps you focus your mind and keep you on track. In the beginning, it might help to be specific. You can write a full list of everything you want to accomplish that day, then check them off as you go. Include small goals, such as, "Don't talk bad about customers."

or "Have compassion." If you really take this suggestion to heart, you might be surprised at how much you accomplish and begin to change for the better. If it helps, look back on your lists and journal entries after a few weeks. I'll bet you'll notice a difference!

Speak Positive Affirmations to Yourself and Others

Words have power—especially when they're coming from the Word of God. Always be positive because what you focus on, you will surely find. Look for ways to serve others by thinking of their needs more than your own. Provide help with a project, buy someone a cup of coffee, offer a listening ear, or speak a word of encouragement. These little things impact everyone, not just you and the person you're helping. Spreading friendship and kindness is contagious.

Remember, you are God's representative in your place of business. You are an ambassador for Christ—a light in the midst of darkness for others. There will always be someone who needs to see God's love and strength through you. Even on days where it might feel difficult to smile or offer help to someone, do it anyway. You'll be surprised how far these kindnesses can go. It's not always easy to be the light amid chaos, but God will never put more on you than you can bear.

Routines are powerful. A simple routine practiced every day, rain, or shine, can become a habit, and habits that are repeated make you who you are. If you're in the habit of gossiping about your co-workers and your boss, chances are you'll be known as a gossiper who has more bad things to say than good. That, in turn, attracts more stress and negativity in your life. The good news is you can change old, unwanted habits, and it's easier than you might think. The trick is to practice new, good habits every day. Your life will change for the better before you know it.

JOURNAL

Contemplations

- ✝ Describe your work environment and include what things you would like to be or feel different.
- ✝ What daily routine or practice can help you create the work atmosphere you want?
- ✝ Start a journal or a daily list. Write out five things you want to accomplish, and list at least one way you can spread a positive attitude.
- ✝ Which scriptures resonate with you to help you set the atmosphere in the workplace? (Following are some scriptures to choose from.)

Scriptures to Reference

Habakkuk 2:3 — "This vision is for a future time. It describes the end, and it will be fulfilled. If it seems slow in coming, wait patiently, for it will surely take place. It will not be delayed."

Hebrews 10:25 — "And let us not neglect our meeting together, as some people do, but encourage one another, especially now that the day of his return is drawing near."

2 Corinthians 5:17 — "This means that anyone who belongs to Christ has become a new person. The old life is gone; a new life has begun!"

Collosians 3:13 — "Make allowance for each other's faults, and forgive anyone who offends you. Remember, the Lord forgave you, so you must forgive others."

Romans 12:2 — "Don't copy the behavior and customs of this world, but let God transform you into a new person by changing the way you think. Then you will learn to know God's will for you, which is good and pleasing and perfect."

Daniel 6:10 — "Now when Daniel learned that the decree had been published, he went home to his upstairs room where the windows opened toward Jerusalem. Three times a day he got down on his knees and prayed, giving thanks to his God, just as he had done before."

PRINCIPLE 3

Redirect Office Gossip

"A gossip betrays a confidence; so avoid anyone who talks too much."

(Proverbs 20:19)

So far, you've started your day by putting on God's armor, then you prepared yourself for work by setting a positive atmosphere, no matter what the day brings. So, what do you do when you've done your part to manage your own attitude and energy but every water cooler in the office is flooded with negative conversations that only bring the company and other employees down? Let's get right to it; gossip is toxic, unconstrained conversation that does nothing but stir up trouble. God warns us to stay away from people who gossip and to guard our own words when we speak about others. Minding your own business and refraining from participating in office gossip will help you avoid the snares of the devil. I Thessalonians 4:11 says, "And to make it your ambition to lead a quiet life: you should mind your own business and work with your hands, just as we told you."

Grace and Bennie

Grace and Bennie were colleagues working for the same organization, reporting to the same manager. They began spending more time together at work as they became better friends. Overall, Bennie was a positive person, but she often shared negative opinions about their manager. For a while, Grace politely listened to Bennie's complaining but tended to let things roll off her back by not getting sucked into the negativity; however, the more Bennie focused her conversation on the rumors she heard about their manager, the more Grace found herself succumbing to gossip and negative comments.

One morning, Grace was in Bennie's office when their manager poked her head in and asked Grace to meet her in her office. As Grace followed her manager to her office and closed the door behind her, she was immediately accused of starting rumors and "talking trash" about her.

Although Grace had participated in Bennie's gossip-starting, she quickly realized what a mistake she had made by not standing up for what she personally believed about her manager and allowing herself to be negatively influenced by Bennie. Through their conversation, Grace found out that much of Bennie's gossip wasn't true. Grace felt a pit in her stomach as she apologized to her manager, knowing she had hurt her feelings and damaged their relationship by trying to fit in with Bennie.

"A good person produces good things from the treasury of a good heart, and an evil person produces evil things from the treasury of an evil heart. What you say flows from what is in your heart."
(Luke 6:45)

It's easy to fall into gossip without even realizing you're participating in it. One comment or response can lead to another and another, and before you know it, you've built a reputation of being a gossiper. Oftentimes, we don't think about what's really sitting beneath the surface of gossip. When someone speaks negatively about another, there's usually a hidden agenda to generate significance for themselves and take it away from the person they're talking about. When it comes down to it, that's a display of that person's own lack of self-esteem and worthiness. It takes true courage to stop gossip when you hear it. The Bible tells us to speak life into our friends and enemies alike because we will reap what we sow. Have you ever heard the phrase "If you don't have something nice to say, don't say anything at all?" You don't have to like every person or even agree with what they do or say but tearing others down by spreading gossip can hurt you just as much as it hurts them.

HOW TO REDIRECT GOSSIP

We've all found ourselves in the middle of gossip, whether starting it, engaging in it, or even spreading it to others. Following are a few ways to "stay out of the gossip pit" in a way that's pleasing to the Lord.

Recognize Gossip

The first step to redirecting gossip is to become aware that you're gossiping! That may sound silly, but it's so easy to be agreeable with someone who shares their opinion with you about another person. After only a couple of comments back and forth, you can find yourself in the thick of a full-blown gossip session.

When this happens, it will feel uncomfortable in your spirit. Maybe you feel uneasy or edgy at the end of the day. You might feel guilty, and you're not sure why. What if you run into one of the people you've been talking about, and you're forced to avoid making eye contact? All these reactions stem from a guilty conscience, or at the very least, the recognition that you might be doing something that could be hurtful to other people. These feelings can leave you feeling uncomfortable, but the first step is to acknowledge them.

Forgive and Forget

If you find yourself engaging in gossip, just remember: if someone is gossiping with you about someone else, chances are they're talking about you, too. Every time someone shares some gossip with you, practice thinking how you would feel if someone spread negative and false information about you. When you feel that little tug in your spirit, the best thing you can do in that moment is to accept it and practice compassion toward the person being gossiped about.

Think back to a time when you may have been the one being gossiped about unfairly. What was your side of the story? Did anyone bother to think of your feelings before spreading a hurtful rumor? Try to avoid the sometimes inevitable "but she did this" or "he said that" or "I wasn't as bad as all *that*." These aren't things for you to justify. It's your responsibility to show love. Then, after you've offered compassion to the person on the receiving end of the gossip, forgive yourself. No one's perfect. These are acts of love toward others and yourself.

Stop It or Redirect It

Stopping gossip can be as easy as simply walking away or changing the subject. Sometimes the best thing to do is smile and walk on. If you can't walk away—and sometimes you can't—redirect. There are subtle ways to do this without making a big scene. Read the situation as best you can and go from there. Change the subject or change the mood. If the gossiper seems wound up and stressed out, address their emotions instead of their gossip. Compassion isn't only for the one being gossiped about. Usually, the person gossiping is in need of some love and healing, too. In redirecting gossip, others will see that you don't succumb to it and will stop trying to pull you into unnecessary drama.

Be the Light

If you feel you are at the center of someone else's gossip, don't fall prey by reacting or retaliating; this just adds fuel to the fire. Avoid entertaining the rumors, and just continue to be a light of love, compassion, understanding, and confidence. God knows the truth of every situation and is standing by to fight your battles in ways that are often unseen. Engaging in negative conversations and rumors is a waste of time and energy. Stand firm in your values so you can be a blessing to others, no matter what the circumstances are.

God wants us to always treat one another with love. Staying clear of office gossip will help you grow a closer relationship with Him as you learn to speak life and positivity into your co-workers. If you keep replacing gossip with a compassionate heart, that anxious, guilty feeling will go away. You'll also find the workplace a much easier, more pleasant place to be.

JOURNAL

Contemplations

- ✝ Take some time to consider what gossiping looks and feels like. How do you define gossip?
- ✝ What things can you do to raise awareness of gossip for yourself and others?
- ✝ In your journal, write about a time when you or someone you love was at the receiving end of gossip. Describe how it made you or your loved one feel. What wasn't true? What do you wish people knew about that situation?
- ✝ Which scriptures resonate with you to help you avoid or redirect gossip in the workplace? (Following are some scriptures to choose from.)

Scriptures to Reference

Ephesians 4:29 — "Don't use foul or abusive language. Let everything you say be good and helpful, so that your words will be an encouragement to those who hear them."

Exodus 23:1 — "You must not pass along false rumors. You must not cooperate with evil people by lying on the witness stand."

James 1:26 — "If you claim to be religious but don't control your tongue, you are fooling yourself, and your religion is worthless."

PRINCIPLE 4

Maintain Your Integrity and Keep the Faith

"So follow the steps of the good, and stay on the paths of the righteous. For only the godly will live in the land, and those with integrity will remain in it."

(Proverbs 2:20-21)

God understands that temptations, obstacles, and challenges are a natural part of life, but if you keep your integrity and have faith, He will absolutely provide. Passage 10:13 in 1 Corinthians says, "The temptations in your life are no different from what others experience. And God is faithful. He will not allow the temptation to be more than you can stand. When you are tempted, he will show you a way out so that you can endure."

In the last principle, I talked about redirecting gossip at work, but that's just one of many actions you can take to maintain your integrity. Integrity is the quality of being honest and having strong moral principles and moral uprightness. As a righteous child of God, you are not broken, empty, nor incomplete. As Proverbs 11:3 says, "Honesty guides good people; dishonesty destroys treacherous people." If you start worrying about all the different ways you can mess up, remember that the Holy Spirit will never guide you in a way that compromises your personal or professional integrity. As a Christian, you are part of a royal priesthood who lives according to the highest standards. It requires you to maintain a level of integrity in every aspect of life.

April

April worked long hours as a loan officer. She often worked 12 hours a day, six days a week, while maintaining a steadfast work ethic and a faithful commitment to her company. She was also known for going out of her way for her customers and extending true kindness and compassion to them. When April's customers faced financial challenges that impacted their ability to make timely payments, she would allow for special arrangements to extend their payment window.

Despite all of this, her manager criticized her work regularly. April received monthly evaluations which included the number of high-interest loans she sold. In a team meeting, April's manager reprimanded her in front of other co-workers for failing to push a customer to take out a larger loan than he could afford.

Still, April refused to compromise her integrity by coercing her customer into taking out a loan she knew he could not repay. Although she was openly reprimanded, she was still able to be at peace with herself because she refused to compromise her integrity. Her cause and purpose were more important than meeting a quota.

> *"This is my command—be strong and courageous! Do not be afraid or discouraged. For the Lord your God is with you wherever you go."*
> *(Joshua 1:9)*

Working in corporate America can involve some competitive situations that will test your moral compass in a big way. In business, and especially the sales industry, it's all about the bottom line, so if you're not producing, you don't eat. Because sales is generally a cyclical profession, you may find yourself as the top salesperson one month and at the bottom for the next. If your family depends on you to make ends meet, stress and anxiety can mount quickly, which makes it even easier to compromise your Christian values and standards. You may have witnessed someone less talented or deserving receive a promotion or advancement because they "play the system" by lowering their standards and compromising their integrity.

As a believer in Christ, there is only one system to play: God's system. There will always be situations in life that tempt you to lower your standards to make others feel comfortable or give yourself a leg up. The good news is that God has made provisions for every situation to work to your advantage! The key is to stay strongly rooted in your relationship with God. As you'll learn more about in Principle 6, there is a season for everything; rest in the knowledge that your harvest is on the way, whether in your current role or in new opportunities you may not even see coming.

Janice

Janice was president and CEO of her own financial company, which was at the mercy of a significant downward shift in the economy that threatened the company's ability to continue operating. Always looking for opportunities to overcome obstacles, Janice went to work to find a solution that would generate more operating capital for the company. She discovered a program which, at first, seemed like the answer to her prayers. As she dove further into the fine print, Janice's hope and excitement quickly dimmed. Her company didn't meet the criteria for the program. In sharing her fear and disappointment with one of her colleagues, they suggested a way to "bend the rules" to qualify.

With the future of her business and that of her employees on the line, Janice was enticed to follow her colleague's advice and apply for the program, even though it meant fudging some numbers. But something held Janet back. She needed to sleep on it before deciding. The next morning, after her prayer and supplication, Janice heard the small voice inside that was discouraging her from applying for the program. Her Chris-

PRINCIPLE 4 | Maintain Your Integrity and Keep the Faith

tian values had taught her to walk upright in her character and her faith. Those same beliefs governed her decision to avoid compromising her integrity. She refused to allow the business that God had blessed her with to be associated with something she knew went against her morals. She decided to forego the opportunity even if it meant the folding of her company. It was one of the hardest decisions she'd ever had to make.

You can see what a difficult situation Janice faced and how blurred the lines may seem when there's a great deal at stake. However, when you allow Christian values to govern you, you will be rewarded with a bigger, better solution than you could ever imagine. In the end, another financial opportunity came along that enabled Janice's company to survive. Had Janice compromised her values, it could have ruined her company's ability to practice. It would have opened the door for the devil to come in and destroy what God had created. The enemy is always waiting for the perfect opportunity to test your integrity through temptation.

Don't Allow Your Integrity to Be Tempted

Perhaps the most obvious story of temptation is found in Luke 4:1-13, when Satan repeatedly tested Jesus while He was fasting and praying in the wilderness for forty days and nights. Although Jesus was hungry, He resisted temptation. Then the devil said to him, "If you are the Son of God, tell this stone to become a loaf of bread." But Jesus told him, "No! The Scriptures say, 'People do not live by bread alone.'"

The devil tried again, saying, "I will give you the glory of these kingdoms and authority over them…I will give it all to you if you worship me." Again, Jesus resisted, saying, "The Scriptures say, 'You must worship the Lord your God and serve only him.'"

In a third try at temptation, the devil took Jesus to Jerusalem to the highest point of the temple and said, "If you are the Son of God, jump off! For the Scriptures say, 'He will order his angels to protect and guard you. And they will hold you up with their hands so you won't even hurt your foot on a stone.'" Jesus countered with "You must not test the Lord your God," and the devil left until the next opportunity presented itself.

Imagine being hungry, tired, and weak, then you are presented with things that would seemingly solve all your problems even though they will lead you down a wrong path. Avoid the temptation to go against what you know to be true and remember how Jesus handled it. Instead of caving in, Jesus used his faith, knowledge, and understanding of God to cast aside these false solutions. Despite his physical weakness, Jesus stayed strong in his faith because He knew His purpose.

Hold on to Your Faith

"Faith shows the reality of what we hope for; it is the evidence of things we cannot see."

(Hebrews 11:1)

PRINCIPLE 4 | Maintain Your Integrity and Keep the Faith

Maintaining your integrity requires staying connected with your faith in God's Divine plan for your life, even when you can't see your way out of a situation, whether at home or at the office. When your back is against the wall, uphold your integrity by holding on to your faith. God will never send you to a place where He has not planted the provision for you to succeed.

We can learn a lot about faith from the book of Daniel. Daniel was a noble Jewish youth of Jerusalem who was taken into captivity for many years serving under several different Babylonian kings. With each trial and test, Daniel upholds his faith and integrity and continues to win people over.

One of his first trials illustrates how Daniel's integrity helped his reputation prosper. He rejected the king's food, prayed to God, and refused to bow to the king's idol. When God gave Daniel insights into visions and dreams, Daniel's prophetic interpretations of the king's dream gave him favor.

Another Babylonian king, King Darius, placed Daniel in a high office, making other officials jealous. So, they plotted against Daniel to discredit him and hired spies to find anything that might arouse suspicion. Still, throughout all his dealings, Daniel was genuine, consistent, honest, and righteous. The spies found nothing. The only way to get him, they said, was to snare him based on his faith.

So, they went to Darius and made a plea. Feeding Darius' ego, they offered to make him a "god" for thirty days. Enacting the law meant that people could only pray to Darius for those thirty days, and the consequences of breaking the law was death. Realizing Daniel prayed three times a day to God, the spies knew this would put him in jeopardy of breaking the law. However, the new law didn't discourage Daniel from his commitment to God. Once he was caught, he was found guilty and thrown into the lion's den.

The point of the story is this: Throughout all the jealousies and accusations, the lies and instability, Daniel remained faithful to God. He didn't back down, no matter what they put him through. He stood strongly for what he believed in.

Our faith in God is non-negotiable. We must learn to live and demonstrate unwavering faith and maintain a high level of integrity, especially during the toughest times. Your enemies are watching your actions, oftentimes observing in judgment, and waiting for you to compromise your values. You'll find that behind the judgment, jealousy, or insecurity lies admiration. There's something to be admired about a person who can endure the pressures of life and stand for what they believe in. You must be ready to lose everything rather than compromise your faith and integrity.

Mark

Mark was a hard-working salesperson with a wife and three children. Over the years, Mark had won many awards for his outstanding work. One day, he was accused by another sales representative of stealing one of his accounts. Mark's manager

PRINCIPLE 4 | Maintain Your Integrity and Keep the Faith

called him into the office to reprimand him for his actions. Mark was distraught. There was no documentation that the account had belonged to someone else. He honestly didn't realize the account was his co-worker's and Mark had already spent a lot of time and effort helping the client.

Even so, the account was taken from Mark and given to the salesperson who claimed the client was "assigned to him," even though he'd never worked on the account. Although Mark was disappointed, he never showed anger; he just let it go because he had faith that God had an even better plan in store for him. A few months later, the other sales representative transferred out of sales and into another position and Mark was promoted to sales manager with his own team.

Maintaining your integrity and keeping the faith is vital to your success in life. It can lead to opened doors you never dreamed of. Integrity will cause your manager to give you that promotion when they see how you can stand up and stand out under pressure. Integrity will cause people to stop and listen to what you have to say because they respect you.

Mark maintained the same integrity at work that he demonstrated in every area of his life. He could have fought the situation by disparaging the sales manager who falsely accused him, but he knew that God would provide in the end. If you hold on to your integrity and faith, God will reward you. Be slow to speak and slow to anger, and let your work speak for itself.

HOW TO MAINTAIN YOUR INTEGRITY AND KEEP YOUR FAITH

You must be led by the spirit every day, even in the workplace. You must remember that your flesh is inadequate. The works of the flesh are a variance to the Holy Spirit. The spirit of the Lord has confirmed you and positioned you where you are today. The flesh will mislead you into thinking that you must react in a manner similar to others. The flesh will convince you that you are not good enough, and if you do not react, you are less than.

Galatians 5:16-17 says, "So I say, let the Holy Spirit guide your lives. Then you won't be doing what your sinful nature craves. The sinful nature wants to do evil, which is just the opposite of what the Spirit wants. And the Spirit gives us desires that are the opposite of what the sinful nature desires. These two forces are constantly fighting each other, so you are not free to carry out your good intentions." I'm making an emphasis on being led by the Holy Spirit because you are going to face some situations in your career where you will encounter confrontation. You want to keep your flesh under control to maintain your integrity.

We've seen too many killings in the news where some disgruntled employee decided to seek revenge by killing co-workers, managers, and innocent bystanders. It's tragic. When a person feels the only way to solve a problem is to kill others, they have lost all hope and faith that there is a positive solution. They have reached the point of destruction, and many times it's self-destruction.

Do you realize, some Christians have thoughts of self-destruction or seeking revenge on others who have harmed them? Some Christians experience wavering if they should tell the truth on an application because they desperately need the job or loan. As long as we live, we will always experience the flesh warring against our spirit. Sometimes you might reach a point where you know the right thing to do, but someone has hurt you so badly that your flesh wants to hurt them back. On the other hand, maybe some of you reading this have never experienced that. As my father would say, "Just keep on a-livin...you will."

The desires of the flesh and the desires of the spirit are not merely different, they are contrary to one another. They are incompatible. The flesh will always lead us to sin, but the spirit leads us to forsake sin and pursue that which is pleasing to God.

How do we keep our faith and integrity? Walk in the spirit by reading God's Word and praying consistently. When Paul wrote to the Colossian believers, he instructed in Colossians 3:2, "Think about the things of heaven, not the things of earth."

When our minds are occupied with the things of this world, we have difficulty keeping in step with the Holy Spirit. On the other hand, when we intentionally think about, dwell on, and meditate on the things of God's kingdom, we find the spirit leading our lives more easily.

Saturating our minds with Scripture has a way of pushing out the things of this world. It will take root in your spirit. What's inside will come out. The spirit will guide you through God's Word daily. You will walk in confidence in God, knowing He has planned for everything to work in your favor. You will no longer feel intimidated by the threat of losing your job. You will no longer doubt your abilities for where you are in your career. You will own the position. This type of confidence can only come through Christ.

Having a lack of confidence, integrity, and faith is a warning against what has been confirmed in the spirit. I've heard this story told in many forms. An older Christian stopped to talk with a new believer, and he asked the young woman how her life in Christ was going. She replied, "It's like I have two people fighting in me all the time—a good one and a bad one. The man asked, "Who wins?" and the woman replied with a grin, "The one I feed the most."

Affirm and Confirm

We have been affirmed and confirmed by God. We must practice activating His affirmations in our lives by speaking them every day. Make it a part of your morning routine before starting your day. The more you say them, the more they will resonate and manifest in your life. Below are a few affirmations you can use. I encourage you to research the Bible and discover more that help you with your Christian walk.

Psalm 23:4 — "Even when I walk through the darkest valley, I will not be afraid, for you are close beside me."

Isaiah 40:31 — "But those who trust in the Lord will find new strength. They will soar high on wings like eagles. They will run and not grow weary. They will walk and not faint."

Ephesians 2:10 — "For we are God's masterpiece. He has created us anew in Christ Jesus, so we can do the good things he planned for us long ago."

Philippians 4:13 — "For I can do everything through Christ, who gives me strength."

Hebrews 13:20-21 — "Now may the God of peace—who brought up from the dead our Lord Jesus, the great Shepherd of the sheep, and ratified an eternal covenant with his blood—may he equip you with all you need for doing his will. May he produce in you, through the power of Jesus Christ, every good thing that is pleasing to him. All glory to him forever and ever!"

Confirmed

You are where you are because you are supposed to be there. God confirmed you for the position you are in and for the life you are living. God gives us confirmation on everything before we know it. He knew you before you were born. You do not need to question if you are supposed to be here. If you are alive, you are supposed to be here. God already knows what He wants you to do in life. If you want to know the will of God for your life, you must start with the word of God. When God gives you confirmation on what He wants you to do, He will show you how to rightly apply the Word of God to your life.

Remember Who You Are

As a Christian, it's important to know who you are in Christ. When you know who you are, you have more control over your flesh and how you react to situations. You think before you speak.

Know your Christian identity and all it entails to live the life God intended for you to live. You can't possibly fulfill your destiny until you know who you are in Christ. You are living at this time for a reason. You are at your present job for a reason. Even if you think it's just for a paycheck, your destiny is bigger than that. The more you agree with God about your identity in Christ, the more your behavior will begin to reflect your God-given identity.

It's so important to see yourself the way God sees you. Do not question when He seats you in high places. God's opinion is the one that counts. Understanding who you are in Christ will give you a strong foundation to build your life upon. Remembering who you are in Jesus is the key to a successful Christian life lived on purpose.

Your identity does not depend on something you do or have done. Your true identity is who God says you are. Once you choose to follow Jesus, the old you passes away and you become a new creation. In 2 Corinthians, Paul tells us that all believers have died with Christ. It was buried with Him, and just as He was raised up by the Father, so are we raised up to "walk in the newness of life." 1 Peter 2:9 says, "But you are not like that, for you are a chosen people. You are royal priests, a holy nation, God's very own possession. As a result, you can show others the goodness of God, for he called you out of the darkness into his wonderful light."

Be Slow to Speak and Slow to Anger

Pause before you react. This is sometimes the hardest thing to do but setting the pause button on an immediate reaction—especially if it's packed with emotion—is sometimes the best thing you can do. If you find yourself being a victim of false accusations, state the facts, and move on. Don't spend too much time trying to defend your truth because the truth will eventually be brought to light. Your strength in handling false accusations will be a witness to others as to how to handle it when they are faced with the same challenges. A negative reaction can cause others to question your character and see you in a less than Godly way. When you hold on to your faith and stand in your integrity, God gets the glory. It also saves you from regretting anything you might have said or done.

There will always be circumstances or situations that will challenge your integrity. Just remember, in corporate America and in life, believers and nonbelievers are watching your actions. Whether you see it or not, they are measuring how you handle conflicts inside and outside the office. The spirit of the enemy is watching and waiting for judgment. You may think one little white lie won't hurt and no one will know, but Satan often uses people to antagonize you to lose your cool and compromise your values.

If you give in and lose your integrity, Satan wins. When you find yourself in a compromising situation, take a moment and think about both the consequences and rewards of your actions. Will you conform to fix the situation, or will you stand for what you believe in? Is it worth losing your credibility if you bend the rules? Will you be missing out on something far better if you maintain your integrity and keep the faith? Pray about it and ask God to let His will be done in your situation, then trust Him. If you believe, it will all work together to benefit you.

JOURNAL

Contemplations

- ☦ Think of some situations that trigger you to lose your faith and integrity. What actions can you take to restore them in those situations?
- ☦ Create at least three positive affirmation statements that will help redirect you to your integrity when tested.
- ☦ List some of your personal core values and describe why they are important to you.
- ☦ Which scriptures resonate with you to help you maintain your integrity and hold onto your faith in the workplace? (Following are some scriptures to choose from.)

Scriptures to Reference

Proverbs 10:9 – "People with integrity walk safely, but those who follow crooked paths will be exposed."

1 Peter 3:16 — "But do this in a gentle and respectful way. Keep your conscience clear. Then if people speak against you, they will be ashamed when they see what a good life you live because you belong to Christ."

Colossians 3:23 — "Work willingly at whatever you do, as though you were working for the Lord rather than for people."

PRINCIPLE 5

Live at Peace with Everyone

> *"Never pay back evil with more evil. Do things in such a way that everyone can see you are honorable. Do all that you can to live in peace with everyone. Dear friends, never take revenge. Leave that to the righteous anger of God. For the Scriptures say, 'I will take revenge; I will pay them back,' says the Lord. Instead, 'If your enemies are hungry, feed them. If they are thirsty, give them something to drink. In doing this, you will heap burning coals of shame on their heads.' Don't let evil conquer you, but conquer evil by doing good."*
>
> *(Romans 12:17-21)*

Living in your integrity and keeping your faith can be tested more than ever in the workplace. We spend many of our waking hours with co-workers who may or may not live according to Christian principles. So, it's of the greatest importance to remember who you are in the Lord when you face deception from others. Deceit means to hide or misrepresent the truth. This may occur in the form of lying, bending the truth, or misleading people. Although we can be deceived by others, we can also deceive ourselves.

Todd and Layla

Todd was a manager no one wanted to work for because he managed his subordinates by using fear tactics. If his leadership was questioned or his authority was challenged, he was known to cheat his team members out of the performance marks they deserved. He also spread negative comments about certain employees to his favorite team members causing unrest among them. Some of the most seasoned and dedicated employees ended up resigning because Todd made their lives so miserable at work. Others stayed, continuing to work diligently despite the hostile work environment, but there was constant complaining about the unfairness in the way Todd managed his team.

One of Todd's team members, Layla, became the brunt of his deceptive behavior when he began spreading false stories about her incompetence as a salesperson. The truth was, Layla was one of the top performers on the team, but she didn't always follow the aggressive sales tactics Todd was teaching, which aggravated him. Todd began spreading lies within the team that Layla was afraid to make cold calls and avoided upselling to her existing customers because she wouldn't follow his sales method. He even told her she wouldn't be a top performer for long if she didn't start following his rules. The truth was, Layla was consistent in her cold-calling and had developed very strong relationships with her customers over the years by building trust and rapport with them gradually, not by aggressively pushing them for incremental business.

When it came time for quarterly performance bonuses to be paid out, Todd and Layla had a meeting where he told her that even though her numbers were good, she may want to consider a job at another company that was a better fit for her selling style. He said, "We don't need salespeople like you." Layla was shocked! She knew he was making negative comments to her team members and felt herself becoming more and more discouraged, questioning her value at her current company, and wondering if maybe Todd was right.

Unsure of what to do next, Layla decided to have a talk with God to find the answer. She prayed for guidance and searched scriptures that would help her find peace for this situation rather than feeling deceived and frustrated.

Very quickly, Layla remembered that God had placed her in her job, and He would protect her and provide for her whether at her current job or a new one. She realized that not only can we be deceived by others, but we can even begin to deceive ourselves in our own minds when we stray from the promises of God. Layla could have believed Todd's negative comments, but instead, she had an awakening in her spirit. She felt a sense of calm come over her and reclaimed her power to stand firm and be a blessing to Todd by praying for him.

As time went on, Todd's threats and comments didn't bother Layla at all. In fact, he began to avoid her altogether, and eventually took a job in another city. Within a couple years of Todd's departure, Layla received a promotion that came with a significant pay increase.

> *"The Lord himself will fight for you. Just stay calm."*
> *(Exodus 14:14)*

At some point, we will all be challenged to deal with situations where we feel unjustly deceived. Whether it's coming from a manager or co-worker, remember that they are either unaware or don't care that their decisions could cause irreparable harm to your career. We can also deceive ourselves when we forget that God has already made plans to prosper us, giving us hope for the future.

But do not be deceived! The co-worker who tried to undermine you is not your enemy. The manager who demeaned you or discredited your performance is not your enemy. Satan is the enemy—the father of lies and deception who is using others to steal or destroy your dreams, goals, aspirations, and destiny.

When you feel attacked or threatened, refrain from becoming intimidated, upset, or vengeful with that person. Keep your peace. Don't waste your time or energy fighting battles you were never meant to fight. Your victory has already been won

PRINCIPLE 5 | Live at Peace with Everyone

and your increase is on the way! If people are talking about you, let them talk. If lies are being told about you, don't feed them; the truth will always prevail in the end. If you believe you've been mistreated, don't give the situation or person your energy. If you feel frustrated or alone on your job, remember that God is omnipotent and omnipresent; He is always right there with you to direct your steps. You have been chosen to be a light and a blessing in the workplace.

HOW TO LIVE AT PEACE WITH EVERYONE

At times, it may seem impossible to live at peace with everyone, but if you have peace within, you will always be at peace. You project onto others what is going on inside you. If you tend to live filled with gratitude and you recognize that everything in life happens for your highest good, you will see things from a fresh perspective.

How do I know everything happens for your highest good? Romans 8:28 says, "And we know that God causes everything to work together for the good of those who love God and are called according to his purpose for them." When you realize everything that happens is working for your good, you don't need to walk around angry or envious because everything is working for your good!

Living at peace starts with you. You must have peace within before you can live at peace with anyone else. How do you learn to have peace within? Remember who you are in Christ.

You will learn this by praying and studying God's word consistently. Through scripture, you will learn God's love and truth on how He trains us to live His way. Through the Word, we are set up for the abundant life God has created for us. When you remember who you are in Christ, you will begin to walk in truth, and you'll be amazed at how you can keep your cool while others are losing emotional control.

Check Back in with How You Wanted to Start Your Day

No matter what's happening in the day, there's a solution. You have the power to remain in control. The workplace can leave you feeling exhausted, which can lead to frustration, causing you to feel overwhelmed and lose your peace. When you experience this, remember you have a place to go. You have a refuge. You can pray to God and ask Him to give you peace and help you focus on your job and not on things that are out of your control.

Taking a moment to ask God for help is not a sign of weakness; rather, it shows your strength and faith that God has everything you need to help you live in peace. We all experience times when our flesh gets overwhelmed. We are human. As humans we have the blessing of going to God and prayer to receive supernatural healing—His peace.

Have a Conversation

If there is an issue that requires your attention, plan to have an open, honest conversation despite it being uncomfortable. Ask a third party to help you resolve the issue. The goal is not to prove who is right or wrong. The goal is to obtain a better understanding.

Take Responsibility

Document your experiences to support yourself. Tell people how you want to be communicated with and respect others in the same way. This is your responsibility. In doing so, the challenges that do arrive will be easier to navigate, less stressful, and more productive for everyone involved.

It's important to understand that your work environment will not always be comfortable, but as a Christian, you have the assignment to be a light to those who are living in darkness. Ephesians 6:12 tells us that we "are not fighting against flesh-and-blood enemies, but against evil rulers and authorities of the unseen world, against mighty powers in this dark world, and against evil spirits in the heavenly places." Offense will surely come; your job is not to fight the battles in the flesh, simply give them up to God. Just as God has empathy for you, you must have empathy for those who challenge you to lose your peace and show them love. Pray for them and watch what God will bring into your life.

JOURNAL

Contemplations

☦ Take a moment to consider a situation that caused you to lose your peace. What about the situation or person involved was so powerful? Once you've finished your reflection, ask God for forgiveness, and give gratitude for the lesson that situation taught you.

☦ What steps can you take to more effectively communicate with co-workers and authority figures?

☦ Write down some of the different ways office politics have caused you stress or anxiety, then consider how you can use Christian values to find more peace.

☦ Which scriptures resonate with you to help you live at peace with everyone in the workplace? (Following are some scriptures to choose from.)

Scriptures to Reference

Ephesians 6:12 — "For we are not fighting against flesh-and-blood enemies, but against evil rulers and authorities of the unseen world, against mighty powers in this dark world, and against evil spirits in the heavenly places."

2 Corinthians 4:18 — "So we don't look at the troubles we can see now; rather, we fix our gaze on things that cannot be seen. For the things we see now will soon be gone, but the things we cannot see will last forever."

Exodus 14:13-14 — "But Moses told the people, 'Don't be afraid. Just stand still and watch the Lord rescue you today. The Egyptians you see today will never be seen again. The Lord himself will fight for you. Just stay calm.'"

Luke 6:27-28 — "But to you who are willing to listen, I say, love your enemies! Do good to those who hate you. Bless those who curse you. Pray for those who hurt you."

PRINCIPLE 6

Let God Handle Your Seasons and Setbacks

"For everything there is a season, a time for every activity under heaven."

(Ecclesiastes 3:1)

In business and in life, there is a season for everything: a season for seed planting, growing, harvesting, and receiving. Each season comes with its own pros and cons. You may be in a season where you feel as though you are not making progress on your job. You may have received a reduction in pay, a demotion, or perhaps even been laid off from work. There are plenty of uncomfortable seasons that may feel like setbacks, leaving you questioning your value as an employee. What may appear to be a setback can be God's way of putting you in a position for something greater.

When you are in an uncomfortable season, you are growing. It's those valley experiences that spur self-expansion. During periods of isolation, you will feel lonely. But you are not alone.

God often uses these times to develop your patience, peace, and maturity.

Jennifer

Jennifer became aware of a position opening in her company. It would be a promotion for her with a substantial increase in pay and boost in her career development. She was thrilled for the chance to move up and make more money and was highly enthusiastic about applying for the job. She confided in a co-worker about her decision to apply. Her co-worker seemed genuinely excited for her. Jennifer made all the necessary preparations and applied for the position. When the announcement was made that Jennifer didn't get the promotion, she later found out the job was given to the co-worker she'd confided in. The one person she'd shared her intentions with was awarded the position because her qualifications ranked higher than Jennifer's. Jennifer felt disappointed and betrayed, questioning, "God, why did you let this happen? I really wanted this job. I needed that money!"

Although Jennifer didn't get that job, God continued to provide. In the end, God placed Jennifer in an even better position. Jennifer came to realize the position her co-worker received included a lot of stress. God protected Jennifer and eventually positioned her in a job with an increase in pay and less stress. God has already provided every stream of revenue, every promotion, and every increase in your life. Don't be concerned about the manipulation of others; God is in control.

When you are faced with what may seem like unfairness or a delay getting your dream job, it's important to remember that seasons are temporary. God knows exactly where you are at this very moment, and He is with you in every aspect of your life. If you feel you're at a standstill, take heart and trust that God is still moving, teaching, and guiding you in preparation for a new season.

In times of suffering, remember Jeremiah 29:11, "'For I know the plans I have for you,'" says the Lord. 'They are plans for good and not for disaster, to give you a future and a hope.'"

This was a message Jeremiah delivered to the Israelites who were held captive in Babylon for 70 years. During their season of captivity, God still promises them that a season of a new future is on the way. In the book of Job, we learn how Job lived in seasons of great wealth and prosperity, as well as seasons where he was stripped of everything he owned, yet he didn't complain. He kept his faith that God had a plan, and his wealth was restored at twice the amount he started with. Even in times when life doesn't seem to be going your way, God has a plan; He has already worked it out!

God Will Turn Your Setbacks into Comebacks

> *"But his brothers hated Joseph because their father loved him more than the rest of them. They couldn't say a kind word to him."*
>
> *(Genesis 37:4)*

The story of Joseph and his brothers in Genesis is another beautiful example of overcoming a temporary setback and turning it into the ultimate comeback. From a young age, Joseph believed God had destined him for greatness. Through his dreams, God assured Joseph that he would rise to a position of leadership over his parents and brothers. From Joseph's point of view, these dreams were evidence of divine blessing rather than his own works or ambition.

From his brothers' points of view, however, the dreams were further manifestations of the unfair privilege that Joseph enjoyed as their father's favorite son. Joseph's failure to recognize this put him at severe odds with his brothers. After initially plotting murder against him, his brothers settled for selling him to a caravan of traders who, in turn, sold him to Potiphar, one of the officials of the Pharaoh. After years of living in slavery, Joseph was called upon to interpret some disturbing dreams of the Pharaoh and was rewarded by being promoted to second-in-command of Egypt! It took a temporary setback to position him in the right place to receive his promotion. Now, that's a comeback!

Sometimes we need setbacks for God to move us into a place to receive a promotion; we'll touch more on that in the next principle. Changes in seasons are necessary and temporary. They are necessary because if you never experience a season of lack, your season of promotion and prosperity wouldn't carry much meaning.

In 2020, the entire planet was faced with the setback of

PRINCIPLE 6 | Let God Handle Your Seasons and Setbacks

COVID-19, a global pandemic that has caused millions of deaths and crashed the economy, which, in turn, put many people out of work. But the turmoil of the pandemic can be viewed another way. During this setback, God gave us time to prepare for a major comeback. Many have chosen to stay stagnant, focusing on how bad their situation is, while others have chosen to learn a new trade, start a new business, research a new industry, or finish an online degree. Setbacks are an opportunity for us to act, knowing that a new season is coming. God has plans for us to prosper!

The greatest setbacks and most challenging seasons have created the most powerful testimonies. Do not be deceived by what you may see as a "permanent setback." There is no such thing. God will see you through every obstacle with a blessing on the other side.

HOW TO LET GOD HANDLE YOUR SEASONS AND SETBACKS

Meet Your Setbacks

If your income has decreased or expenses have increased, learn how to do more with less. Learn how to live on a budget. If you don't know how to create a realistic budget, contact a financial advisor to help you prepare for the next phase in your finances. If you have gained a lot of weight, learn how to eat the healthy way for your body to prepare for a new life. Hire a nutritionist or trainer. If you worked on a job for an extended period and got laid off, prepare for a new job or career. This is an opportunity for you to prepare for a new endeavor. Learn a new skill. Start a business. Start a new career. The opportunities are endless. This will prepare you for the next phase of your life. Prepare for your comeback!

Change Your Perspective

I want to challenge you to look at life from a different perspective. Opportunity is knocking at your door. This is an opportunity to fine tune your craft. If you enjoy your job, learn how to get better at it. Find people who are doing the same job at peak performance levels. If you lose your job, see it as an opportunity to seek out a better one. If you had a desire to become an entrepreneur, this is the time to launch that business. In every season, look for opportunities by trying on a fresh perspective.

Prepare for the Next Season

In preparation for your next season, I encourage you to read more about your areas of interest. Sign up for any training, assistance, or help your company may offer. Search within yourself and ask, "Is this what I aspire to do? Am I operating in my purpose?" If so, discover ways you can become an expert at what you do.

PRINCIPLE 6 | Let God Handle Your Seasons and Setbacks

Setbacks Move Us Forward

It's important to view setbacks as new beginnings. Oftentimes, we look at a period of setback as a final destination. Don't allow yourself to get stuck there. You are merely passing through a phase on your journey that's allowing you to prepare for your next assignment. God has already made provisions for you to reach your destiny.

In times of setback, trust that God is working it out and keep moving. There's a better season on the way!

JOURNAL

Contemplations

- ☩ Look at your career, then determine what season you are currently in when it comes to your job.
- ☩ Identify your career goals and make a list of them. Aim high but maintain realistic goals for each step. Where do you want to be in one year, two years, five years?
- ☩ What skills, experience, and education do you need for each of the goals you've identified? Write down what you can do to get started.
- ☩ Which scriptures resonate with you in allowing God to handle your seasons and setbacks in the workplace? (Following are some scriptures to choose from.)

Scriptures for Reference

Jeremiah 29:11 — "For I know the plans I have for you," says the Lord. "They are plans for good and not for disaster, to give you a future and a hope.

Philippians 4:6-7 — "Don't worry about anything; instead, pray about everything. Tell God what you need, and thank him for all he has done. Then you will experience God's peace,

which exceeds anything we can understand. His peace will guard your hearts and minds as you live in Christ Jesus."
Isaiah 40:31 — "But those who trust in the Lord will find new strength. They will soar high on wings like eagles. They will run and not grow weary. They will walk and not faint."
Hebrews 10:36 — "Patient endurance is what you need now, so that you will continue to do God's will. Then you will receive all that he has promised."

PRINCIPLE 7

Overcome Fear with Faith

"Don't be afraid, for I am with you. Don't be discouraged, for I am your God. I will strengthen you and help you. I will hold you up with my victorious right hand."

(Isaiah 41:10)

In the last principle, you learned that seasons and setbacks are necessary and temporary, but the reality is, setbacks can be scary sometimes. So, what do you do when fear shows up in your spirit? There is a well-known acronym for fear: False Evidence Appearing Real. Oftentimes, we allow that four-letter word to hold us back from pursuing opportunities in our personal and professional life.

John and Shana

John was a manager who had a reputation of bullying employees he didn't like. He created a hostile environment filled with intimidation, condescension, and malicious lies. One of John's employees, Shana, grew more and more anxious because of John's bullying. Each morning before Shana arrived at the office, her stomach became tied up in knots. She loved her job, but she had become a prisoner to her fear of John. Several of Shana's co-workers complained to upper management about John's behaviors, but because John contributed greatly to the company's profitability, they turned a blind eye.

Shana was a Christian and attended church every Sunday. Although she received spiritual strength and wisdom from her weekly worship service, it was overshadowed by her anxiety and fear of returning to work on Monday. One Sunday evening, as Shana was worrying about work, she cried out to God, "I'm tired of the devil beating me up! If you are the same God who delivered Jehoshaphat and his people from a great multitude of armies and delivered David from Goliath, why am I so afraid?"

In that moment, she realized how much power she had given John over her life. She had wasted too many days enveloped in fear. Shana began to pray and speak the powerful Word of God over her life and rebuked the spirit of fear. When Monday morning came, Shana put on the armor of God and walked into work full of peace and confidence. Her anxiety had dissipated, and when she saw John, he suddenly didn't appear as powerful. From that day on, she armed herself with her favorite scriptures every morning before entering her office. Before she knew it, John had no control or power over her emotions.

When Shana decided to use the power God had given her,

PRINCIPLE 7 | Overcome Fear with Faith

her situation at work turned around. She first had to realize who and whose she was, then she had to take her situation to God. As it says in 1 Peter 5:7, "Give all your worries and cares to God, for he cares about you." Shana had forgotten that God's infinite power was always available to her in all situations.

God did not give us a spirit of fear. Fear is only a trick of the enemy. The enemy uses fear to stop us from reaching our destiny; he uses our words to speak fear into our own lives. Shana also realized that it was fear and insecurity that drove John to become a bully to his employees. It was fear that caused him to devalue, discredit, and intimidate others. But Psalm 105:15 warns those who cause affliction: "Do not touch my chosen people, and do not hurt my prophets." No matter what type of bullying you may come against in the workplace, hold your ground and stay in your God-given power.

Consider the story of King Jehoshaphat and his people found in 2 Chronicles 20:15-25. Armies of great multitudes were coming against them, and they were afraid. Jehoshaphat prayed to God for direction, and God responded to him:

> "He said, 'Listen, all you people of Judah and Jerusalem! Listen, King Jehoshaphat! This is what the Lord says: Do not be afraid! Don't be discouraged by this mighty army, for the battle is not yours, but God's. Tomorrow, march out against them. You will find them coming up through the ascent of Ziz at the end of the valley that opens into the wilderness of Jeruel. But you

will not even need to fight. Take your positions; then stand still and watch the Lord's victory. He is with you, O people of Judah and Jerusalem. Do not be afraid or discouraged. Go out against them tomorrow, for the Lord is with you!'

Then King Jehoshaphat bowed low with his face to the ground. And all the people of Judah and Jerusalem did the same, worshiping the Lord. Then the Levites from the clans of Kohath and Korah stood to praise the Lord, the God of Israel, with a very loud shout.

Early the next morning the army of Judah went out into the wilderness of Tekoa. On the way Jehoshaphat stopped and said, 'Listen to me, all you people of Judah and Jerusalem! Believe in the Lord your God, and you will be able to stand firm. Believe in his prophets, and you will succeed.'

After consulting the people, the king appointed singers to walk ahead of the army, singing to the Lord and praising him for his holy splendor. This is what they sang: 'Give thanks to the Lord; his faithful love endures forever!'

At the very moment they began to sing and give praise, the Lord caused the armies of Ammon, Moab, and Mount Seir to start fighting among themselves. The armies of Moab and Ammon turned against their allies from Mount Seir and killed every one of them. After they had destroyed the army of Seir, they began attacking each other. So, when the army of Judah arrived at the lookout point in the wilderness, all they saw were dead bodies lying on the ground as far as they could see. Not even one had escaped.

King Jehoshaphat and his men went out to gather the plunder. They found vast amounts of equipment, clothing, and other valuables—more than they could carry. There was so much plunder that it took them three days just to collect it all!"

Notice they didn't run; they turned their attention away from their obstacle and began to focus on their solution: God! The nature of our warfare is spiritual, not physical; therefore, if the enemy can get us to focus on what our eyes see and not on what the word of God tells us, then he can move us out of our place of peace and power. The more we focus on the wrong thing, the worse it gets. In Psalm 91:2, David writes, "This I declare about the Lord:

He alone is my refuge, my place of safety; he is my God, and I trust him."

Overcome the Grasshopper Mentality

"We even saw giants there, the descendants of Anak. Next to them we felt like grasshoppers, and that's what they thought, too!"

(Numbers 13:33)

In the book of Numbers, Moses sent spies to view the land of Canaan; a land that had been promised to the Israelite people. Even though the land was promised to them, the Israelites were reluctant to claim it because they were afraid. The Nephilim were described as giants, and when the Israelites saw them, they viewed themselves as grasshoppers—weak, small, and insignificant. They saw themselves as potential victims instead of achievers and inheritors of the land God had promised them.

As a Christians, we must guard ourselves against a fearful, unproductive grasshopper mentality. God will guide us in our careers, take care of our families, assist us in finding or keeping a meaningful relationship, and help us manage our finances. The challenge of accepting God's promises may be great, but we must resist developing a grasshopper mentality and have faith that God will deliver on His promises.

Have you declined new opportunities because you felt you weren't qualified? Were you offered a position, wanted to apply, but allowed fear to hold you back? Fear kills opportunities. God wants to give us a better life, but it requires us to have faith that our power to prosper is in the Lord. The enemy can cause us to make things appear worse than they really are, but this is simply an attempt to shake our faith. If we're not careful, we can be used and misled through the words and actions of others, causing us to doubt the power we have in Christ. Remember, when you speak, God is listening, and so is the enemy. We must be mindful to rebuke fear and speak only power and positivity into everything in our lives.

HOW TO OVERCOME FEAR WITH FAITH

Follow God's Instructions Without Delay

There are times when God will instruct you to stand still and be silent. There are also times when God will tell you to speak up and confront an issue. Whatever instruction He gives you, do it without delay! Don't allow your fears to linger into another day because the longer they linger, the worse they become. Fear continues to grow and fester in your thoughts, leading to unnecessary anxiety and stress. Remember, all things are working for your good, no matter how it may look or feel.

See Your Life without Fear

Close your eyes, clear your mind, and visualize who you would be, where you would be, what your life would look like if you had no fear. As a Christian, you are a child of God, a branch of the true vine, a conduit of Christ's life, and a friend of Jesus. You are chosen, holy, and blameless before God, and you've been predestined to obtain an inheritance. (Read Ephesians 1:4, Ephesians 1:9-11, Ephesians 2:10, John 1:12 and 15:1-5, Romans 3:23-24, Romans 6:6, and Romans 8:1-2.)

God requires you to walk humbly with Him. You are to

love and serve Him with all your soul and keep His commandments. (Read Deuteronomy 10:13, Micah 6:8, 1 Corinthians 3:9, and Romans 8:28.)

To combat your fear, remember the reassurances God gives you. Trust that He always has a plan for you. Jeremiah 29:11-13 says, "'For I know the plans I have for you,' says the Lord. 'They are plans for good and not for disaster, to give you a future and a hope. In those days when you pray, I will listen. If you look for me wholeheartedly, you will find me.'"

Be Bold and Take Risks

Whatever the situation in your life or career, you can't allow fear to hold you back. If you are a child of God, there is no reason to fear because God has already created a solution to help you overcome your obstacles. If God has appointed you to be on your job, His grace is there to protect you. Faith is spoken through the tongue, so whatever you speak, your spirit will connect you to it. Just as we find in John 16:33, "I have told you all this so that you may have peace in me. Here on earth, you will have many trials and sorrows. But take heart because I have overcome the world.'"

God says in Malachi 3:5 that He will be "eager to witness against all sorcerers and adulterers and liars. I will speak against those who cheat employees of their wages, who oppress widows and orphans, or who deprive the foreigners living among you of justice, for these people do not fear me."

Trust in God's Word and remember that a great force is working in your favor. So, why are you afraid? Evict the spirit of fear. Apply for that job. Go after that promotion. Ask for a raise. Move, if you need to or start the business you've always dreamed about. You can do, be, and have anything you want, but you must first uproot the spirit of fear so you can thrive in the life that God has called you to live.

JOURNAL

Contemplations

- ☦ What current challenges or obstacles are you facing? What facts support the notion that the challenge is greater than you? What is the root of your fear?
- ☦ What scriptures tell you that God has given you all power to overcome any challenges or obstacles?
- ☦ Which scriptures resonate with you in allowing God to help you overcome fear with faith? (Following are some scriptures to choose from.)

Scriptures to Reference

Isaiah 35:4 — "Say to those with fearful hearts, 'Be strong, and do not fear, for your God is coming to destroy your enemies. He is coming to save you.'"

Joshua 1:9 — "This is my command—be strong and courageous! Do not be afraid or discouraged. For the Lord your God is with you wherever you go."

Mathew 6:34 — "So don't worry about tomorrow, for tomorrow will bring its own worries. Today's trouble is enough for today."

Isaiah 54:17 — "'But in that coming day no weapon turned against you will succeed. You will silence every voice raised up to accuse you. These benefits are enjoyed by the servants of the Lord; their vindication will come from me. I, the Lord, have spoken!'"

PRINCIPLE 8

Be Free of Unhealthy Competition

"Then I observed that most people are motivated to success because they envy their neighbors. But this, too, is meaningless—like chasing the wind."

(Ecclesiastes 4:4)

The atmosphere in corporate America can be highly competitive—sometimes even cutthroat. Often, it's the managers who are driving both healthy and unhealthy competition among their employees to raise production goals. Some employees go to great lengths to be on top, and the rewards can be great if kept in the right perspective. At the same time, constantly comparing your own personal success with that of others can take its toll on you. That's when competition becomes unhealthy. When you focus on your own improvement and becoming the best you can be *for you*, you can run your own race. God has assigned and equipped you for your journey. The vision and purpose God has designed for you is unique to your special gifts.

Rebecca and Jackie

Rebecca and her family had moved to New York where she started a new job. From her first day, she fit right in at the office, laughing and joking around with her co-workers; everyone seemed to love her. As time went on, certain employees noticed that Rebecca was somewhat of a chameleon, acquiescing and conforming her personality to gain favor from whomever she was interacting with at the time. She was especially like this with her managers and was quick to do or say whatever it took to be liked (and hopefully promoted), even if it meant throwing a co-worker under the bus. When it came to building rapport with her peers, Rebecca was easily liked, but she struggled to gain their trust and respect because no one really knew who she was in her full authenticity.

The Bible warns us that an unstable man is unstable in all his ways. Rebecca had an identity issue; she didn't know who she was, so she became whoever she felt others wanted her to be. She had become a pleaser at all costs rather than living in her authentic truth.

Jackie was one of Rebecca's co-workers who had a good reputation and generally kept to herself. Whenever something went wrong in the office, Jackie always looked for a positive way to impact the situation and began getting the attention of her managers as a solid, dependable employee. It wasn't long before Rebecca noticed that Jackie was gaining favor in the office, so in her insecure, competitive nature, she intentionally positioned herself with their managers to plant negative seeds about Jackie. Through the office grapevine, Jackie was tipped off about Rebecca's tactics to turn management against her, but she didn't allow it to distract her from handling her daily responsibilities according to her own personal standards. Jackie stood in her truth; she knew who she was, didn't fear evildoers, and was strong in her faith that her favor would come from God, no matter how she was portrayed by anyone else.

Think and Speak Great Things Over Your Life

"Don't eat with people who are stingy; don't desire their delicacies. They are always thinking about how much it costs. 'Eat and drink,' they say, but they don't mean it."
(Proverbs 23:6-7)

It's the enemy's job to keep the truth from you, to make you feel inadequate, and cause you to believe what others say about you. Satan doesn't want you to know the power God has given you. If you don't know your value and who you are in all your unique gifts and talents, you will never have the confidence to stand boldly in your truth against the attacks of the enemy, which is needed to fulfill your God-given destiny. Satan may use others to pollute your mind with lies that can eventually have you speaking and believing negative things about yourself. What matters is what *you* think and say about yourself.

Do you think you are smart enough and equipped to do your job? Are you settled with who you are? Are you rooted in your personal truth? If you are told you're not a good employee and you believe it, it will surely take root in your life. Taking on the labels others give you means rejecting the person God created you to be.

We are all graced with gifts and talents that are meant to enhance our lives and careers, as well as the lives and careers of others. A gift is something given willingly to someone without any expectation of reciprocation. It can also mean a natural ability or talent. Take a moment to think about the things that come naturally to you—what are you good at? You may find that someone else has a similar gift but no one can do what you do in the same way.

You Can Sink or Swim

I experienced a difficult divorce where I decided to walk away from everything. My finances were plummeting, and I felt myself losing my confidence in the fight to maintain the comfortable lifestyle I had lived for the past ten years. After months of paying attorney fees to get my fair share from the marriage, I decided to let everything go. At that point, the only thing that mattered was my mental stability. I knew if I could maintain my sanity, I was confident I could rebuild my wealth on my own. I realized I had two options: I could sink or swim.

Although I hadn't worked in the media industry for many

PRINCIPLE 8 | Be Free of Unhealthy Competition

years, I made the decision to apply for a job at a local television station. I had already lost virtually all I had; what else was there to lose? The location of the interview was downtown near my existing office. To save gas and time that morning, I packed my interview suit and shoes to change into later. When it came time to get dressed for the interview, I pulled my shoes out of the bag and realized I had packed one navy blue shoe and one black shoe, each with a different height of heel. I began to panic!

Before anxiety completely took control, I stopped, looked myself in the mirror and told myself, "If you believe in yourself and know who you are, these shoes will not stop you from claiming what God has for you. You are more than these shoes! These shoes did not make you; therefore, they cannot break you." I prayed and asked God to calm my nerves and give me peace.

As I walked out the door in my unmatched, uneven shoes, I said to myself, "Remember who you are; God is with you." Peace and confidence quietly settled into my spirit. When I arrived at the interview, I walked toward the general manager's office with my back positioned straight, walking as if I had two perfectly fitted shoes, never once looking down. I continued to repeat in my mind, "Remember who you are, remember who you are." I interviewed with three managers and got the job!

The colleagues in my new career were more experienced, but I wasn't threatened. I knew I had the work ethic that could outperform everyone on the team. I focused on being the best

I could be rather than being better than the rest of my peers. I was my only true competition, and I knew God placed me in that job for a reason. Each year after that, I challenged myself to sell more. For a while, times got pretty tough, and I was forced to get a part-time job to make ends meet, but I was determined not to give up. I knew God had something greater coming. After three years, my sales production at the station increased to the point where I was able to quit my part-time job. Not only did my faith increase, but my salary increased to six figures, and my lifestyle changed completely.

God restored my life. Had I lacked self-confidence and worried how I would look to others, I would have never gone through with the interview. Many times, we limit ourselves and opportunities because we don't know who we are in Christ. We look at others and set expectations based on what others are doing when we should be focusing on the blessing God has given us and the mission we've been sent to accomplish.

Focus on Your Work

> ***"Pay careful attention to your own work, for then you will get the satisfaction of a job well done, and you won't need to compare yourself to anyone else."***
> ***(Galatians 6:4)***

Competition can be healthy, but the competition you have with yourself is much more important than competing with

PRINCIPLE 8 | Be Free of Unhealthy Competition

others. Here's what I mean: sometimes, competing with others is driven from a place of insecurity. People will do everything possible to win because they are seeking significance that's internally lacking due to low self-esteem. Most of the time, those who compete from this perspective are completely oblivious to their behavior. A better way to approach competition is to eliminate the challenge to be better than others and shift to discovering how you can better yourself by building your confidence and establishing the identity you most want to have.

HOW TO BE FREE OF COMPETITION WITH OTHERS

Be the Best at What You Do

In life and in your career, once you've discovered the gifts that bring you the most joy, challenge yourself to become an expert at them! What if you challenged yourself to do more than you did before? If you sold ten homes last month, challenge yourself to sell 20 next month. If you complete six tasks on your to-do list today, challenge yourself to complete 12 tomorrow. Your most important competition is being a better you than you were before.

Focus on Your Own Progress

Companies will often try to encourage competition within its production team or sales staff for increased performance. This is good for the company and for the employee who produces the most, especially if you are in sales. Rather than focusing on what someone else is achieving, focus on doing the job that God has called you to do to the best of your ability. It takes a lot of energy worrying about the progress of others. No matter how fast others are progressing, keep your focus on you.

Have Confidence in God

Believe in yourself and have confidence in God. So many people continue to be disappointed because they put their faith in other people. Don't expect other people to understand your standards or your confidence. Some will embrace you, others will challenge or reject, and that's OK! Be your authentic self. When you realize who you are in Christ, your faith will give you the ability to overcome any situation. God will work it out!

Stay Strong

Workplace competition is a fact of life. Many companies encourage it to fatten up their bottom line, but competition can also be counterproductive and even destructive, resulting in a race that no one really wins. To strengthen your job performance, release the idea that you must compete with others. Likely, their strengths and weaknesses are completely different from yours. Instead, focus on developing your own strengths, skills, and talents. You were hired for a reason. If that reason needs to be improved upon to reach new goals, so be it. The point is to focus on what you can do to improve yourself instead of spending your time comparing yourself to the accomplishments of others. If you start diverting your attention to what they're doing, you're certain to grow frustrated, stressed out, and envious, but if you focus on your own work and goals, you'll develop more confidence and competence.

JOURNAL

Contemplations

- ✝ Take a minute to think about your most positive professional attributes. Why were you hired? What are your gifts and talents? In what ways do you really shine?
- ✝ Now take a minute to think about how to use your skills to improve your overall job performance. Is there anything keeping you from raising your game from good to great?
- ✝ Over the course of the next five days, keep a daily list of all the things you've done well at work, whether it's keeping a customer happy or ensuring a report is accurate. Each day, challenge yourself to go above and beyond your typical level of performance, and continue to add more things you've done well.
- ✝ Which scriptures resonate with you in being free of unhealthy competition in the workplace? (Following are some scriptures to choose from.)

Scriptures for Reference

Galatians 5:26 — "Let us not become conceited, or provoke one another, or be jealous of one another."

Philippians 2:3-4 — "Don't be selfish; don't try to impress others. Be humble, thinking of others as better than yourselves. Don't look out only for your own interests, but take an interest in others, too."

Romans 12:2 — "Don't copy the behavior and customs of this world, but let God transform you into a new person by changing the way you think. Then you will learn to know God's will for you, which is good and pleasing and perfect."

PRINCIPLE 9

Prepare for Your Promotion

"For God is working in you, giving you the desire and the power to do what pleases him. Do everything without complaining and arguing, so that no one can criticize you. Live clean, innocent lives as children of God, shining like bright lights in a world full of crooked and perverse people."

(Philippians 2:13-15)

You just learned that there is no need to engage in unhealthy competition because God has a unique job that's just for you. God gives you desires and aspirations to do things on Earth that will ultimately bring Him glory. It started in the Garden of Eden when God told us to be fruitful and multiply. This command can be applied to every area of your life. You're on your job for a set time and specific reason. While you are there, expect to be fruitful and multiply your wealth!

The pressure to produce more with fewer resources is greater than ever. Employees have debt, families, and other responsibilities that require money to acquire and maintain. The pressure is on. As a result of dealing with this pressure and managing the many responsibilities of life, substance abuse and anxiety medication are on the rise. The good news is that God has already made provisions for you! Before God placed Adam and Eve in the Garden of Eden, He created everything they would ever need to be fruitful and multiply. Psalm 75:6-7 teaches us that our promotions will not come from the East, West, North, or South. They come from God.

Jean

Jean was approached by a corporate representative to move up to management. Despite being in her current position for 12 years, Jean never thought about being promoted; however, the representative had piqued her interest. Jean informed the local manager about the proposal from corporate management, and he immediately dismissed the idea. His response wasn't what Jean expected. He insulted her, saying she wasn't qualified, and that the corporate representative didn't know what they were talking about.

Months later, a management position became available. Jean prayed and asked God for direction. She applied for the job but didn't get it. She was relieved because she'd asked God for His will to be done and was at peace with the outcome. Jean continued to work for her company, not allowing the insult or results of not getting the job affect her work ethic and commitment. She knew who she was, who gave her the job she was in, and who was walking with her. Although her promotion didn't come right away, she knew an increase was on the way. In the years to come, she became the top salesperson in the market and her income surpassed that of local management.

You may be the hardest-working person in the company and never get the recognition you deserve from your manager. Don't internalize it or make it your problem. If God told you to stay where you are, focus on your work performance and how you can improve. It will not go unnoticed forever.

What God has for you is for you, and nothing or no one can change that. The opinions of naysayers don't matter. If your promotion or increase hasn't happened, accept that you are in a time of preparation and trust that your increase is coming.

Down in the Valley

When I started my sales career in advertising, I was flat broke. I was moving through a major transition and was basically starting my life over. I didn't know much about advertising other than there were people making a nice income, and I wanted to find out how I could be a part of a winning team. I pursued a commission-only job, but that didn't scare me. I needed a job. I'll never forget the day I stood in the line at a church on Two Notch Road to receive free food. Neither will

I forget hearing a coworker who was preparing her taxes blurt out in frustration, "I just make too much money!" I had never heard such a thing. Sitting there with barely five dollars in my pocket, I wanted to see what making too much money felt like.

I was also listening to co-workers in their mid-to-late twenties share stories of their elaborate vacations. I had been living in survival mode for at least a year and couldn't even remember the last time I took a vacation. Barely making ends meet, I was inspired to work harder. This season in my life was what the Bible refers to as a "valley experience"—when you're at the bottom and the only way out is up. But I wasn't giving up. I knew I would smile again; I knew I would enjoy life again. I just had to hold on.

My valley experience humbled me. It taught me to budget and the importance of tithing. I knew I could stay in the valley or climb my way out. I continued to excel at my new job and eventually became the top producer on the team. My income increased so much that I was in an upper income tax bracket—the kind where you can say, "I just make too much money!"

Do Not Worry

> *"Don't worry about anything; instead, pray about everything. Tell God what you need and thank him for all he has done."*
>
> *(Philippians 4:6)*

PRINCIPLE 9 | Prepare for Your Promotion

God tests you to increase your faith. You may experience people on your job who don't want to see you succeed, especially when you're exceeding their level of success. Don't be distracted; your promotion is coming. God will reward you for your efforts. The Bible declares that weapons will form against you, but they will not prosper.

In Matthew 6:25, Jesus tells the disciples not to worry. "That is why I tell you not to worry about everyday life—whether you have enough food and drink, or enough clothes to wear. Isn't life more than food, and your body more than clothing? Look at the birds. They don't plant or harvest or store food in barns, for your heavenly Father feeds them. And aren't you far more valuable to him than they are? Can all your worries add a single moment to your life?"

The key to receiving your increase is to first develop your relationship with God, who is the Source of your promotion. God has provided you with all you have and will provide all that's coming.

Colossians 3:23 says to "work willingly at whatever you do as though you were working for the Lord and not people." Your hard work and dedication to the job God has given you will not be wasted or overlooked. If you're in a position where you don't see growth for yourself, ask God for direction. Oftentimes, growth doesn't come the way we expect it to. There may come a time when you're making good money, but you feel a tugging in your spirit that there's something greater for you to do. Ask God for direction, be patient, and trust that He will provide.

HOW TO PREPARE FOR YOUR PROMOTION

Pay Your Tithes

In the Bible, the tithe was an obligatory offering from the law of Moses requiring ten percent of an Israelite's first fruits or harvest. Because God provided the harvest, this part was returned to Him in appreciation for His provision. It was a reminder to the Israelites that all things we have belong to God.

You may already pay tithes and still question if you will ever experience an increase or a promotion. Do not limit increase to a title or increase in pay. You can experience an increase in spiritual growth and in other ways that lead to promotion in ways you never considered.

There were times when I thought I couldn't afford to pay tithes; the truth was, I couldn't afford not to. When I thought about all the ways God had blessed and sustained me throughout my valley experiences, giving back ten percent seemed like a miniscule amount. My increase happened gradually, and through it all, I grew stronger spiritually and deepened my relationship with God.

Prepare Yourself

Prepare and position yourself mentally and physically for increase. One of the worst things that can happen is not being ready to receive your increase when it arrives. Empower yourself by learning more about your area of expertise and become an expert in that area. Seek out the best mentors in your field. Offer to volunteer with an experienced professional who has accomplished what you want to accomplish. Be the person who has already received the increase by feeling grateful for all that's coming. Most importantly, seek God's guidance. This is all part of preparation and positioning yourself for greater things.

Raise Your Standards

Stop wasting time by trying to get others to meet your expectations. Instead, continue to raise your own standards. Eventually, you will meet others who will exceed your expectations. When I started working in a commission-only sales job, I had no experience, but I always had a good work ethic. Work began at 8:30 am. If I arrived after that, I considered that late and not acceptable. Although my colleagues consistently arrived at the office around 8:45, that wasn't my standard. Always strive to be the best version of yourself. Push yourself to produce more than you did the day before. You will be rewarded for your level of performance.

Keep Your Focus on God

Oftentimes, people look for validation according to how much money they make. The Bible tells us not to work hard to be rich. Don't chase the dollar. If you are operating in your purpose, the dollars will chase you. If you seek the Kingdom of God first, everything you need will be provided.

Proverbs 23:4 says, "Don't wear yourself out trying to get rich. Be wise enough to know when to quit." God wants you to be ambitious and prosperous. He doesn't want you to focus only on making money. The scripture goes on to say, "In the blink of an eye wealth disappears, for it will sprout wings and fly away like an eagle." God sees your hard work and commitment, and He will openly reward you for what you have done in secret. David wrote that He will prepare a feast for you in the presence of your enemies.

My friend, you must stand and live according to God's Word. Do the very best you can at the tasks God has given you. Trust Him and know that your increase is coming! Like a fruit that starts out as a small seed, do not despise your small beginnings. Where you are now is not where you may end up. It may seem as if you're not making progress but continue to do your best and watch it pay off. God gives us the ability to increase in every aspect of life. We already have everything we need to do what He has called us to do.

JOURNAL

Contemplations

- ☦ Determine what promotion and increase mean to you. In what areas do you want to grow?
- ☦ What impact would this have on your life mentally, physically, and spiritually?
- ☦ Write down three things you want to achieve at work. Then write down three things from this principle that will help you achieve those goals.
- ☦ Which scriptures resonate with you in preparing you for the promotion God has for you? (Following are some scriptures to choose from.)

Scriptures for Reference

Jeremiah 29:11 — "For I know the plans I have for you," says the Lord, "They are plans for good and not for disaster, to give you a future and a hope."

Proverbs 10:28 — "The hopes of the godly result in happiness, but the expectations of the wicked come to nothing."

Philippians 4:6 — "Don't worry about anything; instead, pray about everything. Tell God what you need, and thank him for all he has done." "

Colossians 3:23-24 — "Work willingly at whatever you do, as though you were working for the Lord rather than for people. Remember that the Lord will give you an inheritance as your reward, and that the Master you are serving is Christ."

1 Corinthians 15:58 — "So, my dear brothers and sisters, be strong and immovable. Always work enthusiastically for the Lord, for you know that nothing you do for the Lord is ever useless."

PRINCIPLE 10

Rest in God

"Then Jesus said, 'Come to me, all of you who are weary and carry heavy burdens and I will give you rest'."

(Matthew 11:28)

Getting a good night's sleep is essential to your health. Proper rest allows your body to rejuvenate and your mind to refresh. Many lie awake at night for hours thinking about all that happened that day on the job and what might happen tomorrow. "I wonder if they will acknowledge me for doing a good job. I wonder if the new manager likes me and sees that I'm an asset. I forgot to send that email." Hours, days, weeks, and months of precious sleep are lost worrying about past events, things that may never happen, or situations that God has already taken care of.

Our bodies need sleep just as it needs air and food to function at its best. During sleep, your body heals itself and restores its chemical balance. Your brain forges new thought connections and helps memory retention. When you deprive yourself of good sleep, your brain and body won't function properly. Lack of sleep can also lower your quality of life and make you more prone to mood swings.

Peter

Peter lived a stressful life. He was always taking care of others. He was a dedicated employee, consumed with daily demands from his customers, managers, and family. He worked in a very competitive environment and was always chasing a deadline. Peter put a lot of pressure on himself to outperform his colleagues. Anxiety ruled his life, and the mountain of stress eventually began to affect his health, leading to sleep deprivation. He was lucky to get a few hours of sleep per night which ultimately affected his performance at work. His attention span was short, and he was often irritable because he wasn't resting.

There are 33 scriptures in the bible that help with rest and calmness. In Matthew 11:28-30, Jesus says to his disciples, "Come to me all of you who are weary and carry heavy burdens, and I will give you rest. Take my yoke upon you. Let me teach you, because I am humble and gentle at heart, and you will find rest for your souls. For my yoke is easy to bear and the burden I give you is light." Jesus is telling the disciples He can handle their burdens. He can handle the stress and demands of the job. He is available to teach you how to handle life *His* way. You can do your job and meet your family needs. Answer the call to live a balanced life and hand your worries over to God.

Giving My Problems to God

Before I truly began giving my problems to God, I suffered from lack of sleep, having conversations with myself throughout the night, recapping events that happened and reenacting ways I could've handled situations differently. It was exhausting!

When I was going through my "valley" experience mentioned in Principle 9, I worried about what people said and thought about me, my failed marriage, my financial situation, you name it. My worries robbed me of countless hours of precious sleep, and it was affecting my performance at work. One day I became fed up and I prayed to God, asking Him for help. Suddenly, scriptures about worrying started to appear in Bible study, church sermons, and conversations. God was speaking and answering my prayer. I had been so engulfed in my woes, I'd stopped reading my Bible and praying, and I wasn't applying His Word to my life. Once I began to incorporate God's principles into my daily walk, my understanding and patience grew, and I began to rest a little better at night.

During my career, I had quarterly evaluations. Although I typically exceeded my goals, I was always nervous and filled with anxiety about my reviews. The night before, I would toss and turn, and the next day I had dark rings under my eyes like a raccoon.

One night, I woke up around 3:00am and couldn't get back to sleep. I decided to read Psalm 23, and afterwards, I got down on my knees and prayed. I finally fell asleep and had a dream about my father who'd passed away nearly 15 years earlier. In my dream, I was preparing a meal for my family, and as I bent down to pick up the barbecue grill, my father reached down to grab it at the same time. "I'll get it," I insisted. Dad looked at me with his hazel eyes and said, "Now Lynn, are you going to let me carry it, or are you going to continue to try to carry it?" We looked at each other and I replied, "Daddy, I'll let you carry it." I woke up and replayed the dream in my head repeatedly. I immediately related it to my anxiety about my evaluation the next day, seeing it as a message from God telling me to let him handle the heavy burden. It was such a comfort to know I could hand my problems to Him. The next day, I got up with praise in my heart, knowing that God was with me, and He had everything under control. And you know what? My evaluation turned out to be exceptional.

I no longer waste my precious time of rest with annoying thoughts about situations that are largely out of my control. Daily challenges and issues at work no longer have control over me. Yesterday is gone and today is a new day. Lamentations 3:23 tells us we are given new mercies every day. Whatever stage you are currently in, you can rest and know that God will not allow you to stumble and fall. You have the power and choice to enjoy every day to the fullest at home and at work.

HOW TO REST IN GOD

Live by the Word of God

The only way to rest in God is to study and live by His Word. What does that mean? Proverbs 3:24-26 says, "You can go to bed without fear; you will lie down and sleep soundly. You need not be afraid of sudden disaster or the destruction that comes upon the wicked, for the Lord is your security. He will keep your foot from being caught in a trap."

As you end your day, read this scripture, then pray and ask God to help you apply it to your life. If something comes into your mind that goes against the words you read, rebuke them. Read the scripture over until it becomes embedded in your spirit. As you remain consistent in applying His Word to your life, it will become a part of you.

Matthew 6:25 says, "That is why I tell you not to worry about everyday life—whether you have enough food and drink, or enough clothes to wear. Isn't life more than food, and your body more than clothing?" Matthew 6:31-34 wraps up the sentiment: "So don't worry about these things, saying, 'What will we eat? What will we drink? What will we wear?' These things dominate the thoughts of unbelievers, but your heavenly Father already knows all your needs. Seek the Kingdom of God above all else, and live righteously, and he will give you everything you need. So don't worry about tomorrow, for tomorrow will bring its own worries. Today's trouble is enough for today."

God knows about everything. It is written that He has provided for you. There's no need to worry about what might happen tomorrow. Rest is needed to be an effective leader for the Kingdom of God. How can you represent God carrying the weight of the world on your shoulders? You have been strategically placed on your job to show the love of God to others, so at the end of each day, give your cares to Him and rest.

JOURNAL

Contemplations

- † What keeps you up at night?
- † What changes are you willing to make to get proper rest?
- † What scriptures will you use to support your commitment to get the rest you need? (Following are some scriptures to choose from.)

Scriptures to Reference

I Peter 5:7 — "Give all your worries and cares to God, for he cares about you."

Proverbs 3:24 — "You can go to bed without fear; you will lie down and sleep soundly."

John 14:27 — "I am leaving you with a gift—peace of mind and heart. And the peace I give is a gift the world cannot give. So, don't be troubled or afraid."

Lamentations 3:22-23 — "The faithful love of the Lord never ends! His mercies never cease. Great is his faithfulness; his mercies begin afresh each morning."

CONCLUSION

I wrote Corporate Christian 101 because I want you to be encouraged. You can thrive in a cutthroat environment without losing your identity. You are working in the world, but you don't have to conform to the ways of the world. I, and many other Christians learned these lessons the hard way. You don't have to compromise your Christian values; just stay true to who you are and stay true to your faith. Always remember, if God has placed you on a job, He has made provisions for you to thrive. Challenges will come. That's why you're there—to grow from challenges and be a light in what can be a dark environment.

There's no reason to give up or lose focus; you are not alone. God sees you and He knows what you're going through. Never allow your career, association, or opinion of others to define you. Your job is what you do; it's not who you are. When you know who you are in Christ, you don't need a title or sign on your office door. God validates and qualifies you. When your confidence lies in God, you can do all things through Christ who strengthens you.

My prayer for you is to grow stronger in your faith and apply these principles to your life. Study your Bible for growth. Your consistent daily actions will serve as a true testament of the peace that God can provide in a toxic or chaotic environment. No longer will you show up Monday morning feeling defeated or anxious. You are victorious because you have put on the full armor of God. When you walk into the office, you can set the atmosphere. Lives will be changed from others watching your ability to handle difficult situations with ease.

Stay away from the naysayers and the gossipers; they will only distract you. Always keep your integrity. Even if you feel like your back is against the wall, maintain your integrity by holding on to your faith. Instead, be at peace with everyone. Be guided by the Holy Spirit knowing God will never place you where He has not planted the provision for you to succeed.

Strive every day to be a better person than you were the day before, and don't make God a last resort. Setbacks may come, but the comebacks are on their way. Let God handle your seasons and setbacks. Overcome your fear with faith. God wants you to prosper but fear can kill opportunities. Remember, you are uniquely and wonderfully made. No one can do what you do the way you do it. The only competition you have is with yourself.

When you have faith that your power to prosper is in the Lord, you can prepare for your promotion, and as you do, keep your focus on God and live according to His Word. Even

CONCLUSION

if it feels like you are not making progress, continue to do your very best because your promotion is coming! Finally, rest in God. Let Jesus handle your burdens, stress, and demands of your job. Sleep soundly and put your cares in God's hands because He's powerful enough to carry them.

I pray this book has blessed you and encouraged you to bless others. Remember to put on God's armor daily—you are a Christian changing the atmosphere in corporate America!

ABOUT VALERIE LYNN RUSSELL

Valerie Lynn Russell is an entrepreneur, marketer, real estate investor, and author. She has worked more than 30 years in corporate America. Her father, Wayne Russell, was an entrepreneur who instilled a strong work ethic in her. After college, Valerie started her corporate career in marketing. She later got her real estate license, opened her own firm, and began investing in real estate. By the age of 30, she was involved in investing, selling, and developing distressed properties.

After a major life setback, Valerie restructured her life by closing her real estate business and returning to corporate America. As she witnessed the challenges of navigating through the stresses of the workplace, she found herself in a position to help others by inspiring them with her personal experiences and spreading the Good News of Christianity. Although she flourished and enjoyed the structure of corporate America, she also realized its ability to both enrich and destroy lives. Friends and co-workers often confided in her about their struggles to survive in their professional jobs. In looking for answers to her dilemmas and those of others, Valerie turned to God.

Valerie holds a South Carolina and Alabama Broker's license, she is a member of the National Board of Realtors, Graduate of National Association of Broadcasters Leadership, and a member of the National Association of Black Journalism. She is also a General Sales Manager working in the Media Industry.

Today, Valerie continues to lead and inspire others through her daily Christian walk in corporate America. She is a coach, leader, and a true woman of God.

Made in the USA
Columbia, SC
25 February 2023

CORPORATE CHRISTIAN 101